T0001863

ESPECIALLY FOR

....

FROM

....

DATE

....

SOAR LIKE EAGLES

SOAR LIKE EAGLES

EAGLES

Devotions for Men

DREW JOSEPHS

BARBOUR
PUBLISHING

Cover Design: Greg Jackson, Thinkpen Design

Published by Barbour Publishing, Inc., 1810 Barbour Drive, Uhrichsville, Ohio 44683, www.barbourbooks.com

Our mission is to inspire the world with the life-changing message of the Bible.

Member of the
Evangelical Christian
Publishers Association

Printed in China.

SOAR LIKE EAGLES

If you've been around the Christian faith for any amount of time, you've probably heard Isaiah 40:31 quoted. Maybe you've even memorized it. . .and if you haven't, it would be a great verse to set permanently in your mind:

> *But those who wait on the LORD shall renew their strength. They shall mount up with wings like eagles, they shall run and not be weary, and they shall walk and not faint.*

In the pages to follow, you'll find 120 devotional meditations based on this powerful scripture. Each reading emphasizes a single word from Isaiah 40:31, drawing out truths from the verse itself, the passage it comes from, and other chapters throughout the Bible. You'll be challenged to view this beloved biblical promise from the perspective of the entirety of God's Word—which is always the best way.

Would you like to run your daily race without weariness? Would you like to walk through life without fainting? Would you really enjoy soaring on wings like eagles, far above the troubles and temptations and terrors of this world? Who wouldn't?

Read on for challenge and inspiration, for the wisdom of the ages that puts your daily struggles into an eternal perspective. Through the prophet Isaiah, God has given us all a gift in the words of this verse. Let's open and enjoy the gift together.

1. WHAT GOES BEFORE

But those who wait on the LORD shall renew their strength. They shall mount up with wings like eagles, they shall run and not be weary, and they shall walk and not faint.

ISAIAH 40:31

Bible teachers have said that when you see a *therefore* in scripture, you should ask what it's there for. The same advice applies to words like *but*.

When a verse begins with *but*, it stands in contrast to what has gone before. In the case of Isaiah 40:31, what went before? A whole chapter contrasting God's utterly unlimited, primary power with humanity's completely finite, secondary abilities. Most immediately, what went before Isaiah 40:31 is verse 30, which reads, "Even the youths shall faint and be weary, and the young men shall utterly fall."

But...

When you make the infinite God your hope, you draw on His power for daily life. You renew your strength. You find the wherewithal to walk and even run through your difficult days. In fact, you will begin to soar on wings like an eagle.

How is that possible? Because the God who created you

also loves you. He is eager to provide the strength you need for any weakness—spiritual, emotional, or physical. Just don't forget the *but*.

The renewal and strength you seek, the walking and running and soaring on wings like eagles are dependent on your hope in the Lord. And that doesn't happen by accident.

Today, make a conscious choice to hope, trust, and rest in God. Acknowledge Him as the creator and overseer of the universe (see Isaiah 40:22 and 26). Recognize His complete wisdom and power (verse 28). Appreciate His special shepherd's care for everyone who follows His Son, Jesus Christ (verse 11).

As you do, you'll find that your strength is growing. Because it's really *His* strength, now turned loose in your life. It's the strength to soar.

It is God who girds me with strength and makes
my way perfect. He makes my feet like the feet
of deer and sets me on my high places.
PSALM 18:32–33

2. AN EXCLUSIVE OFFER

*But **those** who wait on the LORD shall renew their strength.*
They shall mount up with wings like eagles, they shall run
and not be weary, and they shall walk and not faint.

ISAIAH 40:31

Some of God's promises are universal—anyone, regardless of a person's spiritual condition, can enjoy them. Consider, for example, the promise He made after the flood of Noah's time: "While the earth remains, seedtime and harvest, and cold and heat, and summer and winter, and day and night shall not cease" (Genesis 8:22).

But many if not most of God's promises are made to certain people, sometimes in certain places, often in conjunction with certain behaviors. Salvation, for instance, is not universal: "Whoever calls on the name of the Lord shall be saved" (Acts 2:21).

To be clear, there's a universal *offer*: "Whoever desires, let him take the water of life freely" (Revelation 22:17). But each one of us is responsible for our *response*. We must "call on the name of the Lord."

Once we've done that, we still have some obligations to meet in order to enjoy the best of the Christian life—such as the promise of Isaiah 40:31. The renewing of strength and the soaring on wings like eagles is an exclusive offer to "*those* who hope in the LORD."

To be saved takes simple faith. You just believe in Jesus' teaching, death, and resurrection, and God grants you salvation. But to enjoy all His benefits, to "grow in grace" as 2 Peter 3:18 puts it, takes work on your part. If you don't place your hope in God, you won't run and walk and soar. You'll be weary and faint.

But hoping isn't hard. It's not a job for Superman. Any guy can turn his thoughts and his desires and his heart toward God, knowing He's provided many blessings already and promises even more. Like that beautiful ability to rise above.

Why are you cast down, O my soul? And why
are you restless in me? Hope in God, for I shall
yet praise Him for the help of His presence.
PSALM 42:5

3. HE WHOM GOD CALLS

*But those **who** wait on the LORD shall renew their strength.*
They shall mount up with wings like eagles, they shall run
and not be weary, and they shall walk and not faint.

ISAIAH 40:31

Who was Abram that God should call him to found a great nation? He lived in a pagan land, and until God woke him up to his new mission, Abram was probably as ignorant of the Lord as everyone else in his country. He wasn't a consistent first-class worshipper of the Lord—the kind of guy everyone would have expected to be called to such a task. Instead of having earned a place with God, Abram had absolutely no credentials to become the founder of a holy nation. None of his skill sets warranted his receiving the job. At best, he was a baby believer.

Yet God promised this unlikely man that if he followed Him, blessings would follow. And Abram went on a strenuous trip to a new land because he trusted his new God.

Before we come to Christ, we are doubtless as unlikely subjects of God as Abram. We live in ways that are abhorrent to a holy Lord. Solely through his mercy He deigns to have anything to do with us. Yet as with Abram, God calls us to Himself and to our own divine mission, and He sees something in us no one else envisions.

Along with giving us our mission, He provides us with the strength to carry it out, the ability to rise and run the entire race set before us (Hebrews 12:1–3).

In ourselves we could never be worthy of God's call. Instead we rely on the value of His Son, Jesus, whose holiness shines through our ransomed spirits as He uses us to shine His light on the world. In Him we are valuable as we wait on Him.

Now the LORD had said to Abram, "Get out of your country, and from your family, and from your father's house, to a land that I will show you. And I will make of you a great nation, and I will bless you and make your name great, and you shall be a blessing."

GENESIS 12:1–2

4. WE DON'T FAINT

But those who wait on the LORD shall renew their strength.
They shall mount up with wings like eagles, they shall run
*and not be weary, and they shall walk and not **faint**.*

ISAIAH 40:31

As fallen beings living in a fallen world, we are subject to limitations. We are hobbled by the frailties of our fallenness. These cause our physical and mental strength to ebb or even quit altogether. They do the same to our spirit. We are prone to frustration and discouragement and sometimes even to despair. To feel faint means to feel a loss of strength to the point of exhaustion. It can also mean losing heart or losing our will to go on any further due to despondency. Scripture has many examples of people feeling faint.

Elijah is a vivid example. After contending with the prophets of Baal atop Mount Carmel, Elijah faced the wrath of the wicked Jezebel. She threatened to cut off his head for killing her prophets and friends. In dread fear, Elijah fled to the wilderness and sat under a juniper tree. He became so faint and despondent that he pleaded with God for death. Instead God told Elijah He had more work for him to do and would provide the strength he would need to do it.

God never asks us to do something for Him without equipping us for the task. He sent an angel to Elijah to encourage and exhort him. The angel provided Elijah with food and urged him to eat. Elijah would need this sustenance for his journey to Mount Horeb, where God would speak to him.

If we put our hope in God, He promises to provide supernatural strength. Just like Elijah, we'll be propelled far beyond our faintness.

And the angel of the LORD came again the second time and touched him and said, "Arise and eat, because the journey is too great for you." And he arose and ate and drank, and went in the strength of that food for forty days and forty nights to Horeb, the mountain of God.
1 KINGS 19:7–8

5. RENEWAL AVAILABLE

*But those who wait on the LORD shall **renew** their strength.*
They shall mount up with wings like eagles, they shall run
and not be weary, and they shall walk and not faint.

ISAIAH 40:31

The renewal God speaks of in Isaiah 40:31 is not merely a matter of physical strength. We don't need to do a few more pushups or start an exercise program to be more faithful to the Lord.

Certainly, God may give you a distinct physical ability, but that's not all He offers. This verse uses a physical description to get across a spiritual point.

When we come to hope in God, our hearts are cleansed from sin and God makes our spirits new, applying His salvation to our lives. We begin with an initial experience of salvation. As time goes on and we follow His will, our spirits are strengthened. The more we learn of His ways, the more we desire them (Psalm 37:4).

Still, when we face doubts and questions, we can struggle to hold on to our faith and may stray off the path God describes in His Word. Then we need our hearts cleansed from sin and our strength renewed. We need a transforming power to regenerate our lives (Romans 12:2).

Mercifully, God provides us with that change. Once we are saved, He doesn't leave things up in the air. He knows our penchant for falling into sin. So the apostle John tells us: "If we confess our sins, He is faithful and just to forgive us our sins and to cleanse us from all unrighteousness" (1 John 1:9). In the original Greek, the tense of the word translated "confess" imparts the idea that this is not a once-and-for-all confession, but a habitual one. Whenever we sin, God calls us to come to Him, again and again, confessing and asking for His mercy, and He always provides it.

Renewal is always available in Jesus.

Create in me a clean heart, O God,
and renew a right spirit within me.
PSALM 51:10

6. DOES HE EXIST?

*But those who wait on the **Lord** shall renew their strength.*
They shall mount up with wings like eagles, they shall run
and not be weary, and they shall walk and not faint.

ISAIAH 40:31

One might say, "What's the point of worshipping and serving God if we do not believe He exists?" It's a fair question.

How can we know for sure that God does exist? Is there any evidence? Let's examine the natural world and the cosmos we live in for a moment. Science increasingly reveals to us that the universe itself possesses a high degree of order. Many scientists now contend that all this order is the result of a master design that was likely conceived by a very powerful mind. When we consider the complexity of the universe and the intricacies of the human body, can we suppose that all of it "just happened"? How much faith would it take to believe that?

If it is likely that all the wonders our senses perceive came to be because of a very powerful mind, would it be such an unreasonable stretch for us to conclude that the one who possesses that mind has also revealed Himself to us in what we call the Bible? If not, let's take it a step further. If the Bible truly reveals the one who possesses such a powerful and creative mind, does it not also reveal Him to possess a very powerful sense of holiness, righteousness, and love? If so, can we not suppose that the very concept of love originated with Him and ultimately manifested itself in the Incarnation and atoning work of Jesus of Nazareth?

If we agree with this line of reasoning, do we not have before us the most stupendous, incomparable, and superlative object of wonder, love, and devotion we could ever imagine? If the answer is yes, can we do anything but become those who diligently seek Him above all else and everyone else with all our hearts, minds, and souls?

But without faith it is impossible to please Him, for he who comes to God must believe that He is, and that He is a rewarder of those who diligently seek Him.
HEBREWS 11:6

7. WALK IN THE LIGHT

But those who wait on the LORD shall renew their strength.
They shall mount up with wings like eagles, they shall run
*and not be weary, and they shall **walk** and not faint.*
ISAIAH 40:31

Let's go for a long walk.

Knowing God isn't a matter of accepting Him and then walking away. Hoping in the Lord is an ongoing way of life—a long walk with God that won't end until we meet Him in eternity.

What kind of walk will we take? Will we see how much we can get away with, or will we walk close to Him and see Him work in our lives and fellowship with Him? Will we walk in darkness or light? Do our lives show forth His truth or lie about how well we know and serve Him?

God won't give up on you if you fail to walk close to Him, but you probably won't find your Christian life very pleasurable. Dissatisfaction may be a great part of it.

At first, when you walk at a distance, God will try to woo you back to Himself. You may experience a heartbreaking love, much like that of the father for the prodigal son (Luke 15), which shows how much He cares for his disobedient child. But persistent disobedience eventually leads to serious consequences. God will put you in a position in which you will desperately need and recognize Him. This happened to God's people when they disobeyed and were sent into exile in Babylon.

If you want to walk and not faint, don't wait for God to put you in a corner where He has to solve a big problem for you because you haven't walked in His light. Instead walk daily with Him, live the truth, and fellowship with Him. That's not to say you will never have problems. God tests all His children, but those who walk close to Him experience His strength.

Seek Him every day, and have a good, long walk in the light with the Savior.

If we say that we have fellowship with Him and
walk in darkness, we lie and do not live the truth.
1 JOHN 1:6

8. CULTIVATING A RELATIONSHIP

But those who wait on the LORD shall renew their strength.
They shall mount up with wings like eagles, they shall run
and not be weary, and they shall walk and not faint.

ISAIAH 40:31

The dictionary defines *cultivation* as "to foster the growth of." A farmer cultivates his crops. We speak of cultivating or fostering the growth of such things as the arts, racial harmony, and such. How about cultivating a relationship with our Lord Jesus? After all, Christianity is not so much a religion as it is a relationship, right?

In Luke 10, Jesus interacts with a "certain lawyer" who asked, "Master, what shall I do to inherit eternal life?" (verse 25). When Jesus responds with His own question ("What is written in the law?"), the man answers, " 'You shall love the Lord your God with all your heart, and with all your soul, and with all your strength, and with all your mind,' and 'your neighbor as yourself'" (verses 26–27). Jesus replied, "You have answered rightly" (verse 28).

The man's answer sounds more like a command than a mere suggestion. A command can carry with it the notion of knuckling down and getting on with it.

While it's an imperative, we can also see it as an enjoyable and worthwhile pursuit that enriches life. We want to know more about the one who created us and all else our senses perceive. We want to know about His great love for us and why He rescued us from eternal ruin. We want to grow in love for Him and with Him who gives us every good and perfect gift. If so, why not learn more about Him from what He reveals about Himself in His holy, written Word?

As we prayerfully peruse what we read about Him and what He has done for us, He will also communicate with us. He will speak to our hearts and minds, informing us, encouraging us, comforting us, reassuring us, and our hearts will be warmed toward Him. He will draw us to Himself more and more—in good times and not-so-good times. The more He draws us, the more we will want to know about Him and to love Him. We will find that despite all other distractions that vie for our attention, we will want to put Him first before anything or anyone else. He will become our all in all.

My soul longs, yes, even faints for the courts of the LORD.
My heart and my flesh cry out for the living God.
PSALM 84:2

9. LORD OF CREATION

But those who wait on the LORD shall renew their strength.
They shall mount up with wings like eagles, they shall run
and not be weary, and they shall walk and not faint.

<small>ISAIAH 40:31</small>

Who is the Lord? The Bible paints a picture of Him in the earliest pages of scripture as it describes His creation.

Our relationship with the one who, out of nothing, made the heavens and earth and everything in them began in the dust of the earth. From this humble material, God made every one of our body parts and the amazing bits that compose them. Pupils, eardrums, alveoli, blood vessels, organs—all the details of the human body came out of nothing more than dirt. Then God put life into Adam and gave him a spirit that could relate to Himself.

Ponder the work of God in creation, not only for humans, but for all the birds of the air, mammals who walk the earth, and the denizens of the sea, and awe will fill your soul. *Just how did He do that?* you may wonder. *Yet how could He want a close relationship with creations made of dust?*

Despite our unimpressive materials, God calls us to know Him and befriend him (John 15:15; James 2:23). To the God who made elephants and whales, we could seem like small, frail beings, hardly worth His attention, but it is not so. God sees people as the crown of His creation. It makes a difference to Him if we are willing to accept His call, and He cares if we are willing to follow Him.

Clearly, any being with this power is worth knowing intimately. But there is no question about who the stronger one in the relationship is and who should be in charge—if we will let Him.

Are we willing to accept the friendship and lordship of God? Or will we head off in our own direction and walk with lesser friends of infinitely less strength? Will we answer His call or our own?

And the LORD *God formed man from the dust*
of the ground and breathed into his nostrils the
breath of life, and man became a living soul.

GENESIS 2:7

10. HOW *NOT* TO WALK

*But those who wait on the L*ORD *shall renew their strength.*
They shall mount up with wings like eagles, they shall run
*and not be weary, and they shall walk and **not** faint.*

ISAIAH 40:31

In the apostle Paul's various letters, he emphasizes the fact that we take on a new life when we become Christians. He explains how *not* to walk. Unfortunately, we still exist in a sin-sick world and contend with our own sin nature. It doesn't leave us once we start following Jesus, and we cannot get rid of it while we live on earth. Because of this, it is all too easy for us to slip and fall back into sin. We must always be on our guard.

There are certain sinful pitfalls that we must take particular caution against. Paul cites numerous examples in Romans 13:13 when he says, "Let us walk honestly, as in the day, not in rioting and drunkenness, not in sexual immorality and wantonness, not in strife and envying."

Rioting and drunkenness (or drunken revelry) is at best a scandalous exhibition of overindulgence. One yields control of his faculties to liquor, which can easily manifest itself in an altered state of personality—all too often, dreadfully so.

Sexual immorality and wantonness are megaton bombs in their destructiveness. Aside from the damage they do to one's reputation, they also misrepresent and disfigure God's design and intent for human sexuality and His design and intent for sexual intimacy solely within the bounds of marriage.

Strife and envy are two of the most ruinous weapons in the arsenal of human discord. They are the inverse of God's design and intent for interpersonal agreement and social harmony.

All these behaviors scandalize a community of believers of Jesus and bring shame on the offender. The unsaved world is quite unforgiving in passing judgment on Christians who fall into these traps. We are meant to walk in a manner that sets us apart from the unsaved world so we can attract them by our integrity—not repel them by our hypocrisy. We can only accomplish this by prayerfully relying on God's supernatural grace.

You shall not covet your neighbor's house. You shall not covet your neighbor's wife, or his manservant, or his maidservant, or his ox, or his donkey, or anything that is your neighbor's.
EXODUS 20:17

11. PERFECT FAITH

***But** those who wait on the LORD shall renew their strength.
They shall mount up with wings like eagles, they shall run
and not be weary, and they shall walk and not faint.*

ISAIAH 40:31

The Jews of Jesus' day were used to having long lists of rules to follow. Their leaders piled many on earnest Jews. So it was no surprise that Jesus might add something new when he said, "You have heard that it has been said, 'You shall love your neighbor and hate your enemy.' But I say to you, love your enemies, bless those who curse you, do good to those who hate you, and pray for those who despitefully use you and persecute you" (Matthew 5:43–44). This command, which hinged on the word *but*, was a real shocker.

The Jews knew about enemies. They'd had enough of them! And they knew many verses of their scriptures promised God would protect or avenge them. But Jesus put a new twist on Proverbs 25:21: "If your enemy is hungry, give him bread to eat, and if he is thirsty, give him water to drink." Then Jesus went on to expand their understanding, telling them to love, bless, and do good to those who hated and mistreated them.

How could Jesus ask that of them? This made all the difficult rules they'd followed lifelong seem easy by comparison. Then Jesus added: "Therefore you be perfect, even as your Father who is in heaven is perfect" (Matthew 5:48). Now the bar was at its top level, something they could never jump.

Of course Jesus knew that. But He called them to a turning point in faith, in which they understood that all their well-meaning good deeds were as filthy rags (Isaiah 64:6). They couldn't earn their way into heaven; only God's strength and forgiveness could bring them the perfection that Jesus called for. Only sincere faith would make their actions pure.

Perfect faith only comes by His Spirit. It was true then and is true now too. Seek it from Him today.

Looking to Jesus, the author and finisher of our faith, who for the joy that was set before Him endured the cross, despising the shame, and is seated at the right hand of the throne of God.
HEBREWS 12:2

12. UNDER HIS WINGS

But those who wait on the LORD shall renew their strength.
*They shall mount up with **wings** like eagles, they shall run*
and not be weary, and they shall walk and not faint.

ISAIAH 40:31

In the Bible, wings can be a sign of strength when they are connected to a bird of prey. Isaiah 40:31 speaks of those who mount up with wings like eagles, describing the power God gives mere mortals when we trust in Him. It is a pleasing picture. We like the idea of having that power, and we may even rightly seek it.

But that's not the only view of wings that we get in scripture. Psalm 36:7 describes God's strength and the safety it provides by comparing them to the wings of a mother bird caring for her young: "How excellent is Your loving-kindness, O God! Therefore the children of men put their trust under the shadow of Your wings." Cuddled under her wings, chicks are protected by their parent.

God does offer us strength, as the verse in Isaiah promises, and some days we mount up on eagle wings, relying on His power. But we also must recognize and appreciate where that strength comes from and how limited our own is. When life throws harsh difficulties at us, it takes only a moment for us to recognize how much we need God's protection. In a moment, we go from the soaring eagle to the chick beneath mama's wings.

Not every day is a rise-up-on-eagle-wings kind of experience. We are never so powerful that we need not lie under the shadow of God's wings; we never become so fully adult that we don't need His protection. Under His wings, we experience loving-kindness on the hard days that confront us with our own unalterable frailty. Though we may not prefer it, we should recognize that such humbling is a good thing, because if God didn't remind us, we might forget whose strength we rely on and begin to trust in our own. Before long, we'd be in trouble.

Keep me as the apple of the eye. Hide me under the shadow of Your wings, from the wicked who oppress me, from my deadly enemies who surround me.
PSALM 17:8–9

13. WALKING HUMBLY WITH OUR FATHER

*But those who wait on the LORD shall renew their strength. They shall mount up with wings like eagles, they shall run and not be weary, and they shall **walk** and not faint.*

ISAIAH 40:31

Waiting on God gives us strength for those crisis moments when we need to run but also for our mundane, everyday walking. In the Bible, the word *walk* often refers to our daily life experience. That's how the prophet Micah used the term in this familiar scripture: "He has shown you, O man, what is good. And what does the LORD require of you, but to do justice and to love mercy and to walk humbly with your God?" (Micah 6:8).

Helpfully, Micah provides a clear explanation of *how* we are to walk with God.

First of all, He requires us to do *justice*. What does that mean? Fundamentally, it means treating others as we want to be treated—with love. That is scriptural bedrock, and it is derived from the very nature of God Himself. But that is not all He requires of us concerning justice. We are also to defend the rights of others and advocate for them when their rights are being denied or infringed upon. If this is happening, we must speak up on behalf of the victims.

Second, what does it mean to love mercy? *Mercy* can also be translated as "kindness"—and kindness is all about being considerate and generous toward others from a sincere heart. Remember this fundamental truth: you can't be kind toward others if you aren't kind toward yourself (Matthew 22:39). If this is a challenge for you, ask your heavenly Father to help, then allow kindness toward others to grow abundantly out of His answer.

And third, what does it mean to walk *humbly* with God? Humility is the foundation of all other virtues. But consider this: someone has suggested the word *ego* could be an acronym for Easing God Out. We do that through pride, the foundation of all other vices. Let's be honest about who we are based on what God says about us, not what we or anyone else might think.

By living in justice, mercy, and humility, we'll find the blessing of Isaiah 40:31—walking without fainting.

Humble yourselves in the sight of the
Lord, and He shall lift you up.
JAMES 4:10

14. UNIQUE LORD

But those who wait on the LORD shall renew their strength.
They shall mount up with wings like eagles, they shall run
and not be weary, and they shall walk and not faint.

ISAIAH 40:31

As young Solomon dedicated the new temple in 1 Kings 8:23, he described the unique Lord he and his people worshipped: "LORD God of Israel, there is no God like You in heaven above or on earth beneath, who keeps covenant and mercy with Your servants who walk before You with all their heart." The new king and the Israelites who stood before him were surrounded by pagan countries that practiced child sacrifice and other awful rites. Their gods, created of wood and metal by their own hands, had no ability to relate with people personally. Nor could they save a whole nation as Israel's Lord had.

No matter where anyone looked, no other god compared with Israel's. Though human covenants were common in this era, what nation could claim the promises Israel's God had given them? In the midst of endless and painful child sacrifices and fertility rituals that sought to appease pagan gods and make their crops grow, could any other people claim a god of mercy?

When the Lord brought His people into the promised land, those nations must have had an inkling that this God was something different. But they had no expectations of kindly treatment by Him.

What of today? Is there any God like ours? Look at the other offerings out there. Has compassion been an outstanding hallmark of other faiths or cultural ideologies? Have others related to their gods personally, or are they constantly trying to perform in order to get the favor of whomever they worship?

What other religionists can claim that their God was willing to give up His life for them to forgive their sins and establish an eternal relationship with His people?

Take a good look at the Lord who renews you; understand His uniqueness and serve Him with all your heart. He loves You with all of His.

Among the gods there is none like You, O Lord, nor are there any works like Your works. All nations whom You have made shall come and worship before You, O Lord, and shall glorify Your name.
PSALM 86:8–9

15. A STRONG BOW ARM

*But those who wait on the L*ORD *shall renew their **strength**.*
They shall mount up with wings like eagles, they shall run
and not be weary, and they shall walk and not faint.

ISAIAH 40:31

If anyone needed strength in a tough spot, it was Joseph. Betrayed by his brothers, sold into slavery, and falsely accused by a woman who was herself in the wrong, this man was the epitome of someone in a weak position.

But that's not the end of the story. Genesis 49:24–25 reveals what happened next: "But [Joseph's] bow remained in strength, and the arms of his hands were made strong by the hands of the mighty God of Jacob (from there is the Shepherd, the Stone of Israel), even by the God of your father, who shall help you, and by the Almighty, who shall bless you with blessings of heaven above, blessings of the deep that lies under, blessings of the breasts and of the womb."

During his trials, had Joseph been able to hear this blessing his father gave to him as a last gift, he might have wondered if this prophecy would happen. *How*, he might have asked himself, *could my father compare this travesty of a life to a bow—one of the most powerful weapons in the Egyptian army?*

Instead, Joseph heard this blessing following his rise to greatness when he had seen the strength of God working in his life and bringing victory. He had experienced God's faithfulness and could testify to the truths of God's love and His ability to renew a man's strength, even in the most difficult places of life.

Are you tied up in uncomfortable circumstances? God may yet use them to bring great things into your life. Don't despair, but follow Joseph's example. Avoid bitterness, offer forgiveness, and most of all, trust in God to make your bow arm strong.

When God is giving you power against your enemies, you cannot lose.

I bow my knees to the Father of our Lord Jesus Christ
. . .that He would grant you, according to the riches of
His glory, to be strengthened with might by His Spirit
in the inner man, that Christ may dwell in your hearts
by faith, that you, being rooted and grounded in love.
EPHESIANS 3:14, 16–17

16. SON OF THE LIVING GOD

But those who wait on the LORD shall renew their strength.
They shall mount up with wings like eagles, they shall run
and not be weary, and they shall walk and not faint.

ISAIAH 40:31

As others drifted away because they found Jesus' teachings prophesying His own sacrifice too hard, He asked the twelve if they also wanted to leave. Had these, His most faithful men, so misunderstood His Words that He'd lose them too? "Will you also go away?" Jesus asked (John 6:67).

Doubtless, none of them understood what Jesus meant when He had spoken those words that prefigured the establishment of communion, following His upcoming death and resurrection. The twelve may not have known what "eat My flesh and drink My blood" meant, but they knew Jesus and trusted Him. After all, many other of His teachings were less than clear at first, but He had always helped them understand.

Peter spoke up for the group, confirming their faithfulness, saying, "Lord, to whom shall we go? You have the words of eternal life. And we believe and are sure that You are the Christ, the Son of the living God" (John 6:68–69). Really, what was the alternative?

One thing is certain in our lives. We will not always understand the path God leads us down. Jesus' teaching about His death was distasteful to some followers who only wanted the pleasant elements of faith, and they faded away. We, on the other hand, must push through the difficult experiences that help us learn the depths of God's kingdom. With a sure knowledge of the Son and trust that everything that happens is in our Lord's hands, we can be sure that no harm will come to us.

Jesus is our Lord, the Christ, the Son of the living God. There is nowhere else to go. Will we trust in Him to renew us today?

We both labor and suffer reproach, because we
trust in the living God, who is the Savior of
all men, especially of those who believe.
1 TIMOTHY 4:10

17. THE *NOT* OF GETHSEMANE

But those who wait on the LORD shall renew their strength.
They shall mount up with wings like eagles, they shall run
*and **not** be weary, and they shall walk and not faint.*

ISAIAH 40:31

If Jesus is the focal point for our soaring, can we be sure that He is the only Savior of humankind? Can we have confidence that we are on the right course, or is there some other way of salvation?

Interestingly, Jesus asked the same question when He was in the garden of Gethsemane. A fearful dread came over Him. With great anxiousness, He prayed, "O My Father, if it is possible, let this cup pass from Me. Nevertheless, not as I will, but as You will" (Matthew 26:39). In other words, "Is there is any other way that humankind can be saved from Your eternal wrath?" His question was met with silence, but an angel appeared to comfort and fortify Him. Ever thought about that? Humanly speaking, Jesus did not want to die. He did not want to face the horror of crucifixion—a ghastly and painful form of execution. But having received His Father's silent reply, He knew He had to follow through *because there was no other way.*

Is there any other way in our age? The world would have us believe there is. It adamantly declares there are a multiplicity of ways to God, all of them valid, because no one believes in absolute truth anymore. No one has the right to question this position. Really? The world then has overlooked Gethsemane, the question that Jesus posed there, and God the Father's silent response. If there was any other way, His Father would have said it and spared Jesus all the suffering He went through. But He didn't and there's the rub. He did *not* provide any other way, and none will ever exist. It's as simple and as complex as that.

The *not* of Gethsemane is the absolute *yes* of Jesus.

---

*Therefore let us go forth to Him outside the camp,
bearing His reproach. For here we have no
continuing city, but we seek one to come.*
HEBREWS 13:13–14

18. WHO AM I?

*But those **who** wait on the LORD shall renew their strength.*
They shall mount up with wings like eagles, they shall run
and not be weary, and they shall walk and not faint.

ISAIAH 40:31

King David had built himself a beautiful palace, and when it was finished, it occurred to Israel's ruler that this was rather selfish. How could he have a delightful place to live while God was housed in a tent? Shouldn't David build a temple for the God who had been so faithful to him?

The well-meaning king spoke with the prophet Nathan, who quickly told him to start planning. After all, the prophet knew God was pleased with David. Wasn't David a man after God's own heart (1 Samuel 13:14)? It just seemed logical. But that night the Lord visited Nathan and brought all planning to a crashing halt. He reminded the prophet of all the ways He had blessed David and Israel and outlined some plans He had for that nation. But God's plans didn't include a temple built by David.

Clearly, David was disappointed, but when he went before God, he did so in humility. He recognized that he was only king because it had pleased God to put him in that position. "Who am I, O Lord GOD?" he asked (2 Samuel 7:18). Though David seemed to be Israel's ultimate authority, he readily recognized one greater than himself. Graciously, God had let the palace be built before the temple, and it was all part of His plan. David had shed too much blood. His son would build the temple.

If King David humbled himself before God, how much more should we recognize that God is greater than we are? If our plans are redesigned in ways we never expected, who are we to object? Do we dare tell God we know better than He does?

Are we men after God's own heart who humble ourselves before Him, or are we rebellious sons who'd rather have things our own way?

By humility and the fear of the LORD
are riches and honor and life.
PROVERBS 22:4

19. DON'T LOSE STRENGTH

*But those who wait on the LORD shall renew their **strength**.
They shall mount up with wings like eagles, they shall run
and not be weary, and they shall walk and not faint.*

ISAIAH 40:31

Though David fought many battles before gaining his throne, those tests didn't make him doubt God's love and protection. If anything, they proved God's goodness to him. As the Lord sheltered David from destruction, He proved the care He had for the beleaguered king. And David learned that his strength came from the Lord, not his own abilities.

Often, as he and his men hid from King Saul's army, David's situation looked rather bleak. These warriors slipped into hidden places, knowing their enemy could find them at any minute. Perhaps they sometimes wondered why they were fighting and felt tempted to throw in the towel.

But was God good in that joyous moment when He had David anointed as king? Yes. Was He still good when David went to war? Absolutely. Based on those truths, the king could remain confident he would again see better things in his life. David could keep his courage high because his Lord renewed his strength even in the nerve-wracking moments of waiting and the tense times of battles that lay before him.

No matter what David faced, He knew God was greater than any of it. An unfaithful, homicidal king with a trained army coming against David and his followers? The Lord could handle that. David's strength was always girded by belief. Had he and his men relied on their own power, disaster would have followed, but they connected with the one who can never lose. Then they didn't drown their strength in unbelief.

Don't lose *your* strength either. Believe that God is working all things out for your good (Romans 8:28). Patiently set your heart on Him, and see the victories He has in store for you.

I would have lost strength, but I believed I would see
the goodness of the LORD in the land of the living.
PSALM 27:13

20. REJOICE IN WAITING!

*But those who **wait** on the LORD shall renew their strength.*
They shall mount up with wings like eagles, they shall run
and not be weary, and they shall walk and not faint.

ISAIAH 40:31

Waiting usually doesn't take place when you are on vacation, lying on a beach with a tropical smoothie in your hand. It's rarely part of the relaxing times in our lives, and if it were, we wouldn't feel a sense of tension.

More often, waiting is part of a dangerous moment—a time when everything could go wrong, and we need a defense against disaster. That's why, immediately after calling us to wait, Psalm 33 describes God as our defense: "Our soul waits for the LORD. He is our help and our shield. For our heart shall rejoice in Him, because we have trusted in His holy name. Let Your mercy, O LORD, be on us, as we hope in You" (verses 20–22). We await His salvation from disaster, and as we do, we begin to trust that He will come through for us.

Waiting isn't for wimps. It will test the soul and spirit, and it's an exercise of faith. But this trust builder is part of a healthy spiritual life. God doesn't immediately give His children everything they desire any more than a good human parent does. He knows that waiting for a gift may make it more valuable to us—and when we receive everything too quickly, we can become spoiled. God would rather have strong children who trust in Him than ones with unreasonable expectations. That's the way He builds our spiritual lives.

But look at the promise in Psalm 33:21–22 that comes with the waiting: our hearts will rejoice in Him because of the trust that waiting has developed in our lives. As we trust in the God whose nature we know more fully, we rejoice that He is so wonderful. We have experienced His mercy as our hope muscles have been stretched near the breaking point, and we have seen His salvation in our own lives and those of others.

Wait for the Lord, and the joy will come.

I wait for the LORD; my soul waits,
and in His word I hope.
PSALM 130:5

21. WHO LOVES YOU BEST?

But those who wait on the LORD shall renew their strength.
They shall mount up with wings like eagles, they shall run
and not be weary, and they shall walk and not faint.

ISAIAH 40:31

There's nothing in the earth or heavens that doesn't have God's name on it. He owns it all. Who else counts and names all the stars (Psalm 147:4)? Who knows every detail of how the earth works, from its molten center to the last creature who lives atop its crust?

The same incredible God who names every star you see in the night sky knows you by name. He knows your physical attributes, your likes and dislikes, and every detail of the way you are made because He created you (Psalm 139:13).

He put you together and decided to love you and even delight in you (Psalm 149:4 NIV). No one had to twist His arm to make Him like you, and He doesn't like you one day and despise you the next. You were on His mind before you were even born (Psalm 139:16), and even though He knows you aren't perfect, He loves you more deeply than you can even imagine.

This is the wonderful Lord you've committed your life to.

Having a day when you don't much like yourself? God hasn't given up on you. You are worthy of His love. He proclaimed that you are worthy by sending His Son to die for your sins.

Feeling as if God doesn't much care for you? Maybe you really don't like yourself much today. If you have sinned or been drawn away from Him, confess that wrongdoing. Turn from it and recognize and accept His love. Then worship the one who cares for you even more than you care for yourself.

"Behold, heaven and the heaven of heavens belong to the LORD your God, also the earth with all that is in it. Only the LORD had delight in your fathers, to love them, and He chose their descendants after them, even you above all people, as it is this day."
DEUTERONOMY 10:14–15

22. IT MUST BE

*But those who wait on the LORD **shall** renew their strength.*
They shall mount up with wings like eagles, they shall run
and not be weary, and they shall walk and not faint.

ISAIAH 40:31

When a lawmaking body uses the word *shall*, it means "must." If John Q. Citizen "shall" pay an income tax, it must be. There's no getting out of the requirement, no matter how much you might wish you could.

When Isaiah, as God's prophet, wrote, "Those who wait on the LORD shall renew their strength," it must be. There's no way that waiting on the Lord will *not* result in a renewal of strength. It's a guarantee from God Himself.

In our world, we're accustomed to *maybes* and *perhapses* and *mights* and *possiblys*. We often speak in such terms to give ourselves wiggle room if we think we might want to get out of a commitment. But God doesn't work that way. What He says, He does. And what He promises, He fulfills.

Why does waiting on God restore our strength? Because God Himself *is* that strength. The psalms state this truth over and over again: "Do not be far from me, O LORD. O my strength,

You hurry to help me" (22:19). "The LORD is my strength and my shield. My heart trusted in Him, and I am helped" (28:7). "The LORD is my strength and song and has become my salvation" (118:14).

Since God is strength personified, He has the right and the ability to pass that strength along to whomever He chooses. And He chooses to strengthen "those who wait" on Him.

Nobody likes to wait. But you're not going to change most situations on your own anyway—or if you can, it will probably be for the worse. So calm down, quiet down, sit or kneel down before the Lord and wait. Give God time. He will ultimately renew your strength.

---

*"Behold, God is my salvation. I will trust and not be afraid,
for the LORD JEHOVAH is my strength and my song.'"*
ISAIAH 12:2

23. NO REASON FOR SHAME

*But those who **wait** on the Lord shall renew their strength.*
They shall mount up with wings like eagles, they shall run
and not be weary, and they shall walk and not faint.

Isaiah 40:31

Has anyone ever criticized or made fun of you for following God? Perhaps that person called you names, insulted your beliefs, or found other ways to show hostility.

Don't be surprised. If people criticized Jesus when He walked this earth (and they certainly did), people will criticize you too. But if you trust in God, as you faithfully live out the truths of scripture, in time He will give victory over these folks who are really criticizing Him, not you (Matthew 10:24–25).

You may not win any popularity contests with your critics. They may not invite you to their parties. (Would you really want to go anyway?) But instead of sitting in a corner, feeling sorry for yourself, make every effort to love your enemies. Live a consistent lifestyle that waits on God for the victory. Some of your enemies may end up respecting you, even if they don't understand you. Some will always greet you with cruel words. But in the end, they will learn they have more reason to be ashamed than you do.

God never said you will win the battle over your enemies in a moment. You should plan to wait for the long term, expecting that your trust in the Lord will be tested. But also plan on the fact that God will never let you down (1 Kings 8:57). Anyone who goes against God is entering a losing battle (Psalm 37:1–2).

When *you* go into battle, let your weapons include truth, kindness, gentleness, love, and compassion. God's enemies may be vicious, but they are also lost. Your goal isn't to win the battle—God Himself will achieve that—but to reflect His love to the unsaved.

And there is no reason for shame.

O my God, I trust in You. Let me not be ashamed.
Do not let my enemies triumph over me. Yes,
let no one who waits on You be ashamed. Let those
who transgress without cause be ashamed.

PSALM 25:2–3

24. GOD'S *SHALL*

*But those who wait on the LORD **shall** renew their strength.*
They shall mount up with wings like eagles, they shall run
and not be weary, and they shall walk and not faint.

ISAIAH 40:31

The people of Jeremiah's day had plenty of reasons to be sad. God had called them to Himself, but they had preferred their own path of disobedience. After patiently calling them back to Himself for a long time and getting no response, God finally turned them over to their godless lifestyle. When the Babylonians conquered Judah, God's people could see up close and personal what living in a thoroughly pagan society was like. It didn't take long for them to understand how good God was—and how unhappy they would be without Him.

But when they decided they wanted God back, He let them wait for a while. He wanted them to be willing to do the hard things involved in turning from sin.

In the interim between the fervent prayer for restoration in Lamentations 5:21 and God's answer, even the prophet wasn't totally certain God would accept His people's confession. Had He simply had enough? But the prophet was certain of two things: First, if God chooses to restore His people, they *shall* be restored completely; He will act on His will. Second, there was still hope for Judah until the day God told them He would not forgive them. And God hadn't said that.

What *shall* God do for you? As with the people of Judah, He may be simply waiting for your response of obedience. Maybe He wants you to start taking faith seriously and begin doing the things He's told you all along that are part of His will for you. Maybe you have to make a change and show Him you're serious.

You can be certain that God wants to restore you, and He shall do it. Are you willfully getting in the way of the best He has for you? Or are you willing to walk in the direction He has for you now?

But may the God of all grace, who has called us to His eternal glory in Christ Jesus, after you have suffered a while, make you perfect and establish, strengthen, and settle you.
1 PETER 5:10

25. THE CHOICE

*But those who wait on the LORD shall **renew** their strength.*
They shall mount up with wings like eagles, they shall run
and not be weary, and they shall walk and not faint.

ISAIAH 40:31

When God's spirit begins to work in a man's life, he begins to get a new mind. As he grows in the knowledge of Jesus and desires to be like Him, his thinking alters. No longer does sin seem the best way of life. Instead, knowing what God desires of him, that man begins to want to please his Lord. This is renewal.

As our way of thinking is changed by the good and perfect God, we think thoughts that please Him, and our entire lives become new (2 Corinthians 5:17). Then we can follow the command of Romans 12:2 (NLT): "Don't copy the behavior and customs of this world, but let God transform you into a new person by changing the way you think. Then you will learn to know God's will for you, which is good and pleasing and perfect."

To an outsider, a non-Christian, this change might be hard to understand. Many people are confused when a friend or family member comes to Christ. The old person who loved sinful ways seems to disappear. A new being who loves church and scripture and prayer replaces the former person, and that may not appeal to the one who remains in sin. Light and dark do not mix.

The new believer has a choice at that point: be conformed to this world or transformed. Will that person cling to the old ways or give his mind over to Christ for an ongoing renewal from the inside out?

The Christian who tries to return to the world becomes very confused. He can no longer be happy in the old lifestyle because Jesus is working in his heart. Christians are meant to be renewed, and that process started the moment a person chooses Jesus as Savior.

Conformed and unhappy or renewed and joyous in Christ? This is every Christian's choice. What's your response?

For this reason we do not lose hope, but though
our outward man is perishing, yet the inner
man is being renewed day by day.
2 CORINTHIANS 4:16

26. WORKING IN THE RIGHT PLACES

*But those who wait on the LORD shall renew their strength. They shall mount up with wings like eagles, they shall run and not be **weary**, and they shall walk and not faint.*

ISAIAH 40:31

Working for God can easily become wearisome. There is so much to do, so many distressing situations in a world of countless needs and so few solutions.

Many demands crowd our schedules: work, family life, friends, church commitments, and even time for rest from all those needs. What can we turn down? What should we say no to?

How does this kind of life relate to the picture God paints for us in Isaiah 40? How do we run without weariness in the midst of crowded days? Is there some simple solution we've missed? Or was the apostle Paul being overly optimistic when he wrote, "But you, brothers, do not be weary in doing good" (2 Thessalonians 3:13)?

If the Bible commands us not to weary ourselves in doing good, then we must be able to accomplish that. What scripture doesn't say is that we each need to do *every* good thing imaginable. We may not need to accept every service opportunity our church offers. There may be others in the congregation who would do well in those jobs and would benefit spiritually from the work. Maybe we're feeling weary because we're doing things God never intended for us. So let's do only what we can do well without wearing ourselves out. That may leave time for other, more important duties.

Maybe we need to spend more time on the Lord's work and fewer hours on our career. Perhaps that means taking a job that doesn't keep us in the office sixty hours a week.

Whatever God wants us to do, He will provide the energy we need to do it well.

Why not specifically ask God today just what He wants you to do. There's no weariness when we work in the right places.

"But seek first the kingdom of God and His righteousness,
and all these things shall be added to you."
MATTHEW 6:33

27. WALK IN HIS WAYS

But those who wait on the LORD shall renew their strength.
They shall mount up with wings like eagles, they shall run
*and not be weary, and they shall **walk** and not faint.*

ISAIAH 40:31

The image of walking, in the Bible, is a beautiful word picture of progressively advancing toward God.

The people of the biblical age most often went places on foot, often within only a few miles of their birthplace. They had a pedestrian way of life, so when Isaiah spoke of walking and not fainting, people could relate. They had experienced at least a few long, tiring trips on foot on the hot, dusty roads of Judah. They knew the faintness that followed their own exertions.

Psalm writers also used walking as a picture of those who pursued God with consistent obedience. These faithful believers walk so wholeheartedly after God that they avoid sin.

Though we may enjoy many of our days as Christians, this faithful lifestyle is not always a walk in the park. Walking in God's way takes a strength we do not possess naturally, strength to constantly resist sin and do the good things God has in store for us. To fulfill His will, we must walk in His Spirit (Romans

8:3–5). God in us gives us the ability to serve Him wholeheartedly and consistently. In His Spirit, we walk without fainting.

In our world, many would prefer to ride or drive to a destination than to walk. But everyone can understand the value of walking—and God promises blessings to all who "walk" after Him spiritually. Walking, consistently and faithfully, will get us to God's goal. Wait on Him, let Him renew your strength, and you will make progress in His ways.

Blessed are those who keep His testimonies and
who seek Him with the whole heart. They also
do no iniquity; they walk in His ways.
PSALM 119:2–3

28. FOCUS *ON*. . .

*But those who wait **on** the Lord shall renew their strength.
They shall mount up with wings like eagles, they shall run
and not be weary, and they shall walk and not faint.*

Isaiah 40:31

The Sea of Galilee can become quite turbulent. High elevations that ring the lake make it something like a bowl. As a result, air currents trapped within this bowl can suddenly escalate into a full-blown tempest.

Such was the case for Messiah Jesus' twelve apostles when they were crossing to the other side of the lake one evening without Him. On the fourth watch of the night (between 3:00 a.m. and 6:00 a.m.), He approached the boat they were in, walking on a very boisterous sea. The apostles, working hard at the oars because the sea was against them, caught sight of Jesus and took Him to be a ghost. After He'd assured them it was really the Jesus they knew and loved, Peter asked to go to Him on the water. Jesus agreed, and Peter got out of the boat (Matthew 14:28–29).

Now picture it: Peter disembarks onto a raging sea. High waves all about are crashing against the boat. The wind blows furiously. Amid the chaos, Peter begins walking on the water toward Jesus. It's hard to imagine!

Suddenly, though, Peter takes stock of his situation. In a moment, he takes his eyes off Jesus and casts them on the fearful elements all about him. Focus gone, he begins to sink. Immediately, Jesus reaches out, takes Peter by the hand, pulls him out of the water, and says, "O you of little faith, why did you doubt?" (Matthew 14:31). Then they walk together on the water and get into the boat.

We all go through tempests that test our faith. During each one, Jesus calls us to come to Him, regardless of the stress and chaos of the moment. Can we keep a better focus than Peter did?

But we had the sentence of death in ourselves, that we would trust not in ourselves but in God who raises the dead, who delivered us from so great a death and will deliver. We trust in Him that He will yet deliver us.

2 CORINTHIANS 1:9–10

29. DEVELOPING STRENGTH

*But those who wait on the LORD shall renew their **strength**. They shall mount up with wings like eagles, they shall run and not be weary, and they shall walk and not faint.*

ISAIAH 40:31

Have you ever considered what life would be like without God? Many who came to Christ after years of not knowing Him remember what a disaster theirs once was.

If Jesus is not Lord in your life, who or what is? Something must fill the hole in your heart. Will it be another religion or philosophy? Will it be an earthly pleasure that can only end in despair (Luke 8:14)? What kind of strength does this substitute offer? Is there any other faith or idea that offers a rock to stand on? Does another god come alongside to give you strength when you are simply too tired to go on? Can anything else make you perfect?

The God of the Bible gives us a certain amount of natural strength in this life. We are born with physical abilities, which grow as we age, then ebb as old age takes its toll. Hopefully, we develop not only our physical capabilities, but we also strengthen our minds and emotions and the spiritual gifts He gives us. God doesn't give us strengths and abilities for no purpose. He expects us to use them to advance His kingdom. We need to develop all of His gifts, but unless we depend on His power, we may never make the most of them and use them in the best ways.

May we always remember that every good and perfect gift (James 1:17) comes from Him. Instead of becoming proud of our abilities, let's humbly acknowledge Christ as their source. When we use the strength He's given us to advance His kingdom, everybody wins.

For who is God, except the LORD? And who is a rock, except our God? God is my strength and power, and He makes my way perfect.

2 SAMUEL 22:32–33

30. "BUT THOSE" PEOPLE

But those who wait on the LORD shall renew their strength.
They shall mount up with wings like eagles, they shall run
and not be weary, and they shall walk and not faint.

ISAIAH 40:31

Believers seem to be the *but* of scripture, the people for whom things change. Isaiah 40:30 says, "Even the youths shall faint and be weary, and the young men shall utterly fall." In limited human power, men fail, even those who appear strong. The *but* of Isaiah 40:31 turns that expectation around. Those who wait on the Lord, that is, believers, are those who renew their strength.

John 1:11–12 contains another *but*: "He came to His own, and His own did not receive Him. *But* as many as received Him, to them He gave power to become the sons of God, even to those who believe in His name." Jesus came into the world, and the typical human response was rejection, even though He was the light sent by the Father. In Him was a life force like nothing else anyone had seen on earth. You might have thought men would be rushing to His side to experience this new life. Yet relatively few responded.

Christians are the exception to this broken world's rule. They are the *but those* of whom God speaks in Isaiah. Men who do not know God are limited in their strength, however powerful they appear. They are deprived of His supernatural energizing that the *but those* have access to.

Do you feel as if you are a very ordinary Christian? Recognize that you are an exception, one of the *but those*. You could have been one of those who rejected God's gift of His Son, who sacrificed Himself for your sins. But God called, and you received Him. There is nothing ordinary about that. That choice made you a son of God, not by your own ability, but by His grace and power. As His child, He gives you salvation and access to His strength.

You have been purchased at a tremendous cost—the blood of God incarnate!

But you are a chosen generation, a royal priesthood,
a holy nation, a special people, that you should
declare the praises of Him who has called you
out of darkness into His marvelous light.

1 PETER 2:9

31. WAITING ON GOD

*But those who **wait** on the LORD shall renew their strength.*
They shall mount up with wings like eagles, they shall run
and not be weary, and they shall walk and not faint.

ISAIAH 40:31

If you read the books of the minor prophets, you'll see that God repeatedly took His people to task for the injustices that had become common in the nations of Israel and Judah.

Hosea 12:6 is written mainly to the northern kingdom of Israel: "Therefore, return to your God. Keep mercy and judgment and wait for your God continually." God called that nation back to Himself, a change they would show by living in a combination of mercy and proper judgment, a lifestyle that would have changed their whole society. Instead of taking advantage of others, they would be kind to them and do what was right. For Israel's decadent lifestyle, it would have been a huge change. And it would have shown they loved the Lord.

We often live the wrong way because we want everything quickly. It was true in Old Testament times and it's true today. If we have a problem, we want an answer now. Solutions must be instantaneous, or we worry and sulk. So to avoid anxiety and despondency, we may rush off to find our own way around the problem. That's what ancient Judah and Israel did when their enemies threatened them—a very bad choice with worse consequences. Alliances with Assyria and Egypt would not solve their political problems, and lying to God wouldn't keep them from judgment (Hosea 12:1–2).

It's not that God doesn't want us to be problem solvers. But our best solutions come from Him and are based on His truths. When we run ahead of Him, we can find ourselves deep in a swamp of new problems. That's why God calls us to wait. When we live faithfully for Him, loving the Lord our God and seeking His timing, we have proper judgment and mercy in our decision-making. This greatly pleases our Lord.

Waiting may seem stressful, but it's the best solution—because God is our best problem solver. Looking for His solutions makes life run much more smoothly.

My soul, wait for God alone,
for my expectation is from Him.
PSALM 62:5

32. WHEN ENOUGH IS ENOUGH

But those who wait on the LORD shall renew their strength.
They shall mount up with wings like eagles, they shall run
*and not be **weary**, and they shall walk and not faint.*

ISAIAH 40:31

Sometimes we feel we have been pushed to our very limits, and living is more than we can bear. At times like these, everything about life makes us weary. We feel as though we don't want to take another step. Just one more burden, however slight, will cause us to scream, "That's it. Enough is enough!"

In times like these, we need God's restorative strengthening. More than that, we need to know that God cares about us. It may seem to us (as it did to Job) that God has distanced Himself and is not listening. But that's not true. Our Creator and almighty Father is closer to us than we realize, and He is listening, particularly in wearisome times. "Well," you may ask, "if He really is there, and He really is listening, then why doesn't He just pull me up out of all my weariness and misery?" Languishing can be a real test of our faith. Like Job, we want answers, and we want out of our circumstances *now*!

Though it may sound like a hollow cliche, God will not give us more than we can bear—with His support, of course. And He has a purpose for each trial He permits us to face. Our weariness is not without reason or profit in His plan for us. Could our Father be trying to teach us something that might not register otherwise? Could He be using trials to demonstrate His supernatural providence in strengthening us, helping us to persevere as an inspiration and testimony to others?

Remember, God's ways are not our ways (Isaiah 55:8)—and it is difficult for us to determine the *why* behind His motives. That's where a prayerful trust in His promise never to leave or forsake us (Hebrews 13:5) is our sure lifeline.

"My soul is weary of my life. I will leave my complaint on myself. I will speak in the bitterness of my soul."

JOB 10:1

33. WALKING IN THE LAW

But those who wait on the LORD shall renew their strength.
They shall mount up with wings like eagles, they shall run
*and not be weary, and they shall **walk** and not faint.*

ISAIAH 40:31

What does it mean to walk in the biblical sense? Metaphorically, it means to consistently follow a certain course of conduct in one continual direction. As Christians, we are called to follow the example set by Jesus and walk as He walked. That means deliberately conforming our conduct to the example He set and the truths He taught about a life that is pleasing to our almighty Father.

Sure, we are all infected with a sin nature that is self-centered and bent on taking us off course. Besides this, we live in a fallen world that is dead set against God and His law. It is a world that wants no part of Him or anyone who professes to believe in Him and serve Him. The evil that pervades this fallen world is all around us, and we as Christians are still susceptible to its attraction and pull.

Thankfully, Jesus has saved us from hopelessness, from being chained to our sin nature. We need not be slaves to it. Despite our proneness to sin, we can still live a life that is undefiled, free of corruption. How? Because of something theologians call "The Great Exchange." When Jesus hung His head in death on the cross, He took our sins on Himself and gave us His righteousness. Though we still fall and fail, we are covered by the righteousness of the Messiah and thus made righteous by Him.

Now we are moved to walk humbly before our gracious heavenly Father, knowing we have done nothing to earn such a tremendous and undeserved gift. This realization pushes us to walk ever more faithfully and obediently before our Father, growing in His all-power-filled grace to overcome our sinfulness in the process. The psalmist called this walking in the law of the Lord.

Blessed are those whose way is undefiled,
who walk in the law of the LORD.
PSALM 119:1

34. WAIT ON THE LORD

*But those who **wait** on the Lord shall renew their strength.*
They shall mount up with wings like eagles, they shall run
and not be weary, and they shall walk and not faint.

ISAIAH 40:31

Waiting on the Lord isn't like waiting for a bus. When you stand at the corner, watching for your ride, you know what to expect. The transportation company has a schedule, so you know when the bus should appear, and if it doesn't, you know it will be along soon. You know how much you'll need to pay, that you will need to take a seat (or stand during rush hour), and you know just where the bus is going. If you travel frequently at the same hour, you may even get to know some of your fellow travelers. Even if you don't know their names, you can identify some as the woman with the beautiful long red hair or the man who always has his son with him.

Waiting on God seems less predictable. The schedule isn't yours; it's His. He doesn't post it anywhere. And the road may be less than smooth and turn in a direction you didn't expect. Unlike your bus trip, waiting on God takes courage. It may even feel like a less-than-enjoyable adventure at times.

God tells us we will need courage to travel on His itinerary, but He promises to strengthen our hearts for the journey. Would He call us to do anything He also wouldn't give us strength to complete? Never! As we trust in Him, we find our spirits lifted. We know He will never desert us (Hebrews 13:5), and we can trust that He knows every highway and byway we will travel. Traffic snarls won't stop us if we remain patient and believe in Him. He will get us to our expected destination: heaven.

If God's "bus" seems late or the ride a bit wild, stick around. Don't run off willy-nilly in search of another option. Wait on the Lord for renewed strength. . .and a guaranteed arrival at the right destination.

Wait on the Lord. Be of good courage, and He shall strengthen your heart. Wait, I say, on the Lord.
PSALM 27:14

35. REDEEMING OUR TIME

But those who wait on the LORD shall renew their strength.
They shall mount up with wings like eagles, they shall run
*and not be weary, and they shall **walk** and not faint.*

ISAIAH 40:31

We all have only twenty-four hours in a day. Time is a precious commodity. Once it's gone, it's gone, and there is no retrieving it. How best should we spend our time as disciples of Jesus? A better way to ask this is to say, "How best should we *invest* our time?"

Investing means we're seeking a beneficial return—not for ourselves but for our King. If we say we're investing our time, then it makes sense to be careful about the way we do it. We invest our time by the way we walk.

In this verse, *walk* means how we behave. As followers of Jesus, we're to walk carefully. This means ordering our conduct so it conforms to our Lord's example. Life is filled with traps, and our adversary knows just how to set them for each one of us. We must then walk circumspectly, which means with continual vigilance, staying on track with our thinking and behavior.

We're to walk as those who are wise, that is, skilled in the practical application of knowledge as revealed in God's Word.

We're to skillfully apply our knowledge of His revelation to the day-by-day situations we encounter. How wisely we deal with our circumstances determines our destination.

As disciples, we should also make the most of our time as we walk. This is the apostle Paul's idea of "redeeming the time" (Ephesians 5:16). Let's plant seeds of witness for Jesus as we go. Preach the gospel both with your conduct and then your words. Simply put, lead by example. You may be surprised how many doors God will open for you to share your faith.

See then that you walk carefully, not as fools, but as wise, redeeming the time because the days are evil.
Ephesians 5:15–16

36. THE SHADOW OF HIS WINGS

But those who wait on the LORD shall renew their strength.
*They shall mount up with **wings** like eagles, they shall run*
and not be weary, and they shall walk and not faint.

ISAIAH 40:31

While Isaiah 40:31 shows a vivid image of what men can do when they are powered by God, this verse is not scripture's only imagery of wings.

Even believers who mount up on eagles' wings can find themselves in a dangerous place—a place where they need to avoid enemies who do not know God and would destroy any work that moves His kingdom forward. Perhaps they need to escape a sin that would destroy their own lives. So Christians need another set of wings—God's protective wings.

Even while God freely offers to share His strength with us and encourages us to take advantage of it, He knows it probably won't be permanent. Only as we stay constantly in His will can we rise up on those eagle wings. If an errant wind pushes us off course, we are likely to lose the smooth air current we were riding a few moments before and tumble back toward earth.

The strength to soar comes from God, not ourselves. He knows our weaknesses and the diversions that often send us in other directions. We need help and we need it often; God knows and generously provides it. So the Bible also gives us this picture of protective wings, a place of safety for our times of weakness.

The warrior-psalmist David didn't take this need to live in the shadow of God's wings as an insult. He understood that, compared to God, he had no strength to speak of. The shadow of God's wings became a place to rejoice in because God loved David enough to protect him.

God loves you too. Your rightful place is under His wings. Don't get caught up in your own frail power, forgetting that all the power in this world is God's. Just be thankful He offers you both power *and* protection.

Because You have been my help, therefore in the shadow of Your wings I will rejoice.
PSALM 63:7

37. GOD'S INVINCIBLE WORK

*But those **who** wait on the LORD shall renew their strength.*
They shall mount up with wings like eagles, they shall run
and not be weary, and they shall walk and not faint.

ISAIAH 40:31

We can be certain of this: once God has begun something, He will carry it through to completion. He tells us through the prophet Isaiah that His word will not return to Him void but will accomplish what He intended for it to do (Isaiah 55:11). Speaking through the apostle Paul, our almighty Father says that He will sustain us to the very end of our lives so we will be able to stand blameless before Jesus when He appears (1 Corinthians 1:8). Once our Father makes us alive in Jesus, we become new creatures (2 Corinthians 5:17). From that point forward, He conforms us, step by step, into the very image of His Son (Romans 8:29). He accomplishes this through a process called *sanctification*.

What is sanctification? It is a continual, progressive transformation in our entire being whereby we are inclined to live in a manner that honors and pleases our Father. Though our sin nature does not die and continually seeks to pull us away from God and back into sin, His transforming power overrides this negative power and ultimately triumphs (Romans 7:18–25; 1 John 4:4). Our Father accomplishes this through the wondrous work of the Holy Spirit who works within us, moving us to walk in the righteousness of Jesus. Jesus gives us His righteousness in exchange for our sin, the effects and eternal consequences of which He destroyed through His sacrificial death on the cross (2 Corinthians 5:21).

What a kind and loving heavenly Father we have! He has not only sacrificed His Son to spare us from His fearful wrath against sin, but He has also given us the indwelling work of the Holy Spirit through whom we are conformed to the very image of His Son. Because of Jesus, and in spite of our sin, our Father brings those who wait on Him home—safely and without blame.

He who has begun a good work in you will
perform it until the day of Jesus Christ.
Philippians 1:6

38. RELY *ON* GOD

*But those who wait **on** the Lord shall renew their strength.*
They shall mount up with wings like eagles, they shall run
and not be weary, and they shall walk and not faint.

Isaiah 40:31

In aviation, pilots are taught to rely on their instruments. In fact, the safety of their passengers depends on how well they work with and trust those instruments. And when weather totally obscures the visibility of pilots, they have no choice but to trust the instruments. Not doing so would be fatal. Human limitations suddenly become all too apparent. The proven reliability of the instruments gives pilots confidence in depending on them.

We have a God whose trustworthiness has been proven for eons and is without parallel. He sees the big picture, from beginning to end. He sees what we cannot see and knows what we do not know.

Nowadays, we hear the phrase "I've got this," and there is something to be said about self-reliance. But that only goes so far. It isn't always the surest way. We like to pride ourselves in thinking we know best until our judgment goes awry in this, that, or another situation. If we claim allegiance to God, who is omniscient, why not depend on Him for all guidance and direction? He has endowed us with an ability to think through situations and challenges and determine correct solutions for them. He expects us to use this ability He has given us, and though He will never force us to, He eagerly wants us to seek His guidance and direction and walk with Him. If we choose not to, we run the risk of stalling—or worse.

Our almighty Father has His ways of guiding and directing us, first and foremost through His manual for life and living, His written Word. In addition to this primary source of guidance, He might also counsel us through others or situations or circumstances. Though if we suspect that God is speaking to us through these, it is always best to double-check with Him in prayer and His Word just to make sure.

We can count on His trustworthiness. He can be relied on.

Trust in the LORD with all your heart and
do not lean on your own understanding.
PROVERBS 3:5

39. HUMILITY AND STRENGTH

*But those who wait on the LORD shall renew their **strength**.*
They shall mount up with wings like eagles, they shall run
and not be weary, and they shall walk and not faint.

ISAIAH 40:31

When we think of strength, perhaps muscles come to mind. Yet one of the Bible's best descriptions of strength involves a desperate woman with rock-hard *faith*.

Hannah wasn't a picture of power when she traveled to Shiloh to ask God for a child. She described herself as afflicted (1 Samuel 1:11) and pled with God for help. Hannah had probably followed the advice of the midwives to try to beget a son, yet everything had failed. She was a picture of frailty and hopelessness.

But one hope remained for Hannah: God. Though she could not manipulate life to conceive a child, she knew the issue wasn't entirely in her hands. She went to Shiloh and humbled herself before the altar.

God heard Hannah's humble, desperate prayer. He gave her a son that she had promised to return to the Lord if He so blessed her. Hannah followed through on her promise and gave

Samuel into God's service. Then she spoke prophetically of the Lord's strength and His ultimate judgment through the Messiah (1 Samuel 2:2–10).

Some of Hannah's words were doubtless based on her own experience, but all of them show understanding of her own weakness and the Lord's great power. We don't know Hannah's physical size and strength, but she was towering in her belief in the God of Israel. She understood that He could take even the frailest person and make him or her powerful. In God's almighty hand, even stumblers can be strengthened beyond anything they ever imagined.

Does your strength lie in rock-hard muscles or the biblical Rock?

---

*I was strengthened as the hand of
the Lord my God was upon me.*
Ezra 7:28

40. LIGHT AFFLICTION?

*But those who wait on the LORD shall **renew** their strength.*
They shall mount up with wings like eagles, they shall run
and not be weary, and they shall walk and not faint.

ISAIAH 40:31

"We are troubled on every side, yet not distressed; we are perplexed, but not in despair; persecuted, but not forsaken; thrown down, but not destroyed," Paul proclaimed in 2 Corinthians 4:8–9.

In the first century, life was very hard for Christians. You might compare it to the current-day difficulties of faith in the Middle East, where being a Christian brings persecution and often even death. Paul and his fellow believers also put their lives on the line for Jesus. They were despised by the Jews and persecuted by their Roman rulers, who followed multiple pagan gods and worshipped the emperor.

Paul knew he could die at any time either from persecution or normal human frailty, but he didn't see that as a problem. "For we who live are always delivered to death for Jesus' sake, that the life of Jesus might also be made evident in our mortal flesh" (2 Corinthians 4:11). Living for Jesus brings many kinds of death, but supernatural faith overcomes suffering and even physical death. As long as his life testified to Jesus, Paul was winning.

As he suffered, the apostle experienced both a continual spiritual renewal and the hope of eternal rewards. "Knowing that He who raised up the Lord Jesus shall also raise us up with Jesus" (2 Corinthians 4:14), he referred to his earthly sufferings as "light affliction" (2 Corinthians 4:17). Compared to knowing and serving Jesus and spending eternity with Him, what could the world offer? Death simply meant Paul would meet Jesus sooner. The great apostle might have been endangered on the outside, but inside his spirit was undaunted.

What light affliction of suffering seeks to turn you from God? Remind yourself of the ongoing inner renewal that comes by your faith in Jesus. Like Paul, you cannot lose.

Put off, concerning the former conduct, the old man,
which is corrupt according to the deceitful lusts,
and be renewed in the spirit of your mind.
EPHESIANS 4:22–23

41. A CERTAIN ETERNITY

*But those who wait on the LORD shall renew their strength. They shall **mount up** with wings like eagles, they shall run and not be weary, and they shall walk and not faint.*

ISAIAH 40:31

"Mounting up" on eagle wings sounds great. But the Bible describes another kind of mounting up—the rise of the wicked in their arrogance. Happily for us as Christians, it is limited in its life expectancy: "Do you not know this of old, since man was placed on earth, that the triumphing of the wicked is short, and the joy of the hypocrite but for a moment? Though his arrogance mounts up to the heavens, and his head reaches to the clouds, yet he shall perish forever like his own dung" (Job 20:4–7).

Some people think they're good enough, smart enough, strong enough, whatever "enough" to reach heaven. But God is quick to shoot down such thoughts: "The LORD looked down from heaven on the children of men to see if there were any who understand and seek God. They have all turned aside; they have all together become filthy. There is no one who does good, no, not one" (Psalm 14:2–3).

God makes it very clear. Even our best attempts at righteousness are like "filthy rags" (Isaiah 64:6). And a perfect God cannot tolerate the slightest taint of sin. It's utterly repulsive to Him. So how can we relate to the God who made us? Only through His grace and mercy, which made a way through the sacrifice of His Son. In our borrowed perfection, which comes from trust in Jesus, God warmly accepts us.

The wicked don't last forever. They may seem to triumph for a while, and we may not even see their downfall in this life. But God's long-term view is what really counts, and the success of wickedness on earth will not continue into heaven.

Be grateful that God has spoken His truth to your heart. Humbly accept His generous offer of salvation. Put your trust in Him for every earthly need, and make Him the center of your life. . .and you will mount up on eagles' wings to heaven.

Jesus Christ, whom having not seen, you love. Though now you do not see Him, yet believing, you rejoice with joy unspeakable and full of glory, receiving the result of your faith, even the salvation of your souls.

1 PETER 1:7–9

42. WHO ARE YOU?

*But those **who** wait on the LORD shall renew their strength.*
They shall mount up with wings like eagles, they shall run
and not be weary, and they shall walk and not faint.

ISAIAH 40:31

Jesus' mother and brothers came to speak to Him as He was preaching, and His disciples let Him know His family was waiting.

From such an ordinary situation, Jesus helped the crowd understand how important they were to Him. Though He surely loved His earthly family, they were not the only ones who mattered. Mary and her other children's claims on Jesus were not more urgent than those of the obedient followers before Him. And since not all His brothers believed in Him—at least at one point (John 7:5)—some of Jesus' hearers might have been *closer* to Him than His brothers.

How wonderful was that truth for the people who sat before Jesus—that they were loved like His next of kin. How sad for those brothers who grew up with Him and couldn't see the promised Messiah right before their eyes.

Those people standing before Him in the first century are

not the only ones Jesus regards as family. If you have received Him yourself, *you* are God's son (John 1:12). And Paul explains, "For as many as are led by the Spirit of God, they are the sons of God" (Romans 8:14). If you are God's son, Jesus is your brother, perhaps even more than your own earthly siblings.

The next time you feel you are not important to God (Satan whispers such lies in believers' ears), remind yourself that He chose you as His child. You, His adopted son, have a place with the Father, through His redemptive Son, and you are His heir (Galatians 4:4–7).

Who are you? A child of the King. So live as He commands. Be led by His Spirit. Do His will today and make your Dad proud.

"Who is My mother? And who are My brothers?"
And He stretched out His hand toward His disciples
and said, "Behold, My mother and My brothers! For
whoever does the will of My Father who is in heaven,
the same is My brother and sister and mother."
MATTHEW 12:48–50

43. WAITING AT THE GATE

*But those who **wait** on the LORD shall renew their strength.*
They shall mount up with wings like eagles, they shall run
and not be weary, and they shall walk and not faint.

ISAIAH 40:31

Are you on the lookout for God? Or have you become less vigilant in watching for Him?

The book of Proverbs gives us a picture of a guard, alert and waiting at his city's gate with expectation. "Blessed is the man who hears me, watching daily at my gates, waiting at the posts of my doors" (Proverbs 8:34). Every day he keeps to his post, looking for God to appear on the road or in the hills around his city. He listens for every sound of his Lord's coming.

The idea of an alert watchman is not just for the soldiers of Jerusalem; Proverbs calls us to be alert to our King's appearance, watching for it every moment.

Of course we live in expectation of Jesus' second coming. We may think of it, wish for it, and talk about when it may happen—what prophecies have been fulfilled, and what still must take place—but are we also ready for the appearance He makes in our daily lives? When we pray, are we alert to whatever

He is telling us? Do we listen to discover His will for us each day? When there's a need to obey, are we ready for His call to action, and do we see His work in our lives and the missions He has for us?

Have we remained on guard, ready for His call? Or are we nearly sleeping at our post? Are we like the five faithful virgins of Matthew 25, ready for our Bridegroom, or like their unprepared sisters?

Consistent waiting is not easy. Getting up and going to church when we feel weary is challenging. Regular scripture reading may elude us at times. But let's not sleep at our post or walk away from the gate. The King is coming, and our Lord promises a blessing for those who wait for Him, those who are ready when He appears.

Even so, come, Lord Jesus.
REVELATION 22:20

44. SHEPHERD-KING

*But those who wait on the **LORD** shall renew their strength.*
They shall mount up with wings like eagles, they shall run
and not be weary, and they shall walk and not faint.

ISAIAH 40:31

In one of scripture's most well-known passages, God describes Himself as a shepherd.

Does that seem an odd way for God to picture Himself? Shepherding wasn't the most honored job in Israel. It was messy and smelly, caring for silly animals who got into trouble and couldn't get themselves out of it. Shepherds were out in all kinds of weather, and the job didn't have a lot of perks. Youths and the elderly most often served in the role.

The best a shepherd could hope for was that the sheep would come to know him and perhaps have some affection for him. Maybe they'd even follow the shepherd out of trouble.

That actually sounds like the job Jesus took on when He came to save us from our sins.

We couldn't eradicate sin from our own lives. Being the Messiah wasn't a comfortable mission from the Father. All the benefits came to us because Jesus was willing to be the good shepherd who put His sheep before His own comfort. He left heaven to do this messy job with the confidence that His work would be worth it in the end.

Goodness and mercy are ours because Jesus took on the hard task. We get to enter heaven because He suffered. And one day, in a final reward that makes it all worthwhile, He will rule as Lord over the whole earth (Revelation 17:14).

Until that day, will we acknowledge Him as Lord and serve the one who came to serve us? Will we seek His blessing, not that of the world? We not only serve a powerful God; we serve the "good shepherd," who "gives His life for the sheep" (John 10:11).

What can He ask of us that we would not be willing to do?

The LORD is my shepherd. I shall not want. . . . Surely goodness and mercy shall follow me all the days of my life, and I will dwell in the house of the LORD forever.
PSALM 23:1, 6

45. FAITH FINISHER

But those who wait on the LORD shall renew their strength.
*They shall mount up with wings like eagles, they shall **run***
and not be weary, and they shall walk and not faint.

ISAIAH 40:31

We all run what the writer of Hebrews sees as an Olympic-style race of faith, in which we are surrounded by believers who have gone before us (Hebrews 12). Will we run without weariness?

What keeps us from running successfully? Does sin hold us back? If so, put it off (Ephesians 4:22, Colossians 3:8)!

We sometimes feel that sin is impossible to put aside. Perhaps it has held on to us for many years. . .or maybe we just love a sin too much to part with it. Compulsions are strong, but just as a runner puts aside poor habits and trains rigorously to win the race, we should do the same. Let's be willing to seek God's help to avoid the stumbling block of sin. Then let's resolutely deal with the habits that impede us from reaching our finish line.

As we run, we can count on discouragement and doubts. Our course is not easy. But we have one asset any would-be medal winner lacks—a Champion who has run the race before us. He runs with us, encouraging us moment by moment, giving us the strength we need to win. Greater than any coach, Jesus builds our spiritual muscles so we can cross the finish line into His kingdom.

With a cloud of witnesses to cheer us on and Jesus by our side, we have all we need to run victoriously.

Do you not know that those who run in a race all run,
but one receives the prize? So run, that you may obtain it.
1 CORINTHIANS 9:24

46. QUICK RESCUE?

But those who wait on the LORD shall renew their strength.
*They shall mount up with wings like **eagles**, they shall run*
and not be weary, and they shall walk and not faint.

ISAIAH 40:31

Did eagles swoop down and whisk the enslaved Israelites out of Egypt? No. We know they walked out of bondage because scripture records the event. God is speaking poetically in Exodus 19:4 where He says, "You have seen what I did to the Egyptians and how I bore you on eagles' wings and brought you to Myself." But that doesn't lessen the truth that He bore them out of Egypt quickly, as if they had flown away. His rescue was sudden, swift, and effective, like the flight of an escaping eagle.

God wasn't just creating a reputation for pulling Israel's irons out of the fire when they felt uncomfortable. He was looking for a relationship with the people, and He gave the Israelites this promise: "Now, therefore, if you will indeed obey My voice and keep My covenant, then you shall be a special treasure to Me above all people. For all the earth is Mine" (Exodus 19:5).

God may help us out of difficult situations too. He *may* become the eagle that lifts us out of trouble in a moment, but

He's more than a life preserver on a rope. He wants relationship more than a quick rescue.

The Lord might even let us stay in a difficult place if that will draw us closer to Him. Think of the Jews during their Babylonian exile: had God immediately sprung them from bondage, they would have felt better in the short term, but they probably would have gone back to their sinful ways in a month. The Lord wanted to emphasize their need to come to Him *and stay with Him*. They had to appreciate His rescue.

God didn't lift the Israelites out of every distasteful problem. He's unlikely to do so for you either. But know this: if He hasn't rescued you yet, He has a purpose.

Lord, how long will You look on? Rescue my soul from their destructions, my dear life from the lions.
PSALM 35:17

47. EVICT THE SQUATTER

*But those who wait on the LORD shall **renew** their strength.*
They shall mount up with wings like eagles, they shall run
and not be weary, and they shall walk and not faint.

ISAIAH 40:31

An escape from sin. Oh, what a wonderful spiritual prospect!

And that's just what God says we have—the ability to put off our old nature and live in a renewed way that transforms us. We will be new people, no longer bound by our own wrongdoing.

Knowing God makes the difference. We can't put on His image if we don't know Him. And even if we've begun to know Him, we won't put on that new man if we hold on to particular sins.

But when sin really hurts, when we get tired of trying to do things our own way, when we have seen what harsh paths our disobedience leads us down—then God has our attention. We can't wait to put off the old man, who has become simply an uncomfortable squatter in our spiritual life. Deep down, we know that since God has come into our lives, sin should no longer have a place. But too often we open the doors of our lives and find our unwelcome guest waiting for us.

Evicting the old man takes effort. He'll act as if he owns the place, but that changed entirely once we accepted Christ. Our "house" belongs to Jesus now (Romans 6:6).

Though the old man pops up, perhaps incessantly, we really have been renewed. We no longer need to live in our old, sinful ways. But we must intentionally put off the old man and put on the new one every day. Will we live in God's truth or let that squatter take over? The amount of renewal we enjoy is largely our own choice.

Don't lie to one another, seeing that you have put off the old man with his deeds and have put on the new man, who is renewed in knowledge according to the image of Him who created him.
COLOSSIANS 3:9–10

48. PRESCRIPTION FOR STRONG FAITH

*But those who wait on the LORD shall renew their **strength**.*
They shall mount up with wings like eagles, they shall run
and not be weary, and they shall walk and not faint.

ISAIAH 40:31

Toward the end of the letter addressed to them, Paul urged his Philippian readers to live a successful Christian life. Residing in a prosperous Roman colony, these believers had wrestled with a "Judaizing" influence—the argument of some that said Christian men should be circumcised and still follow the Old Testament Law.

The apostle knew that was not the best way to follow Jesus, and he outlined what really makes for successful Christian living in chapter 4, verses 4–9—not rule following, but grace. Paul advised the Philippians against following the Law but told them they should rejoice in the Lord, be gentle with others, not be anxious but pray in every situation, and give God praise with thanksgiving; they should focus on true, noble, right, pure, and lovely things and put His teachings into practice. "And the peace

103

of God, which passes all understanding, shall guard your hearts and minds through Christ Jesus" (Philippians 4:7).

Would Paul's prescription for a successful Christian life be easy? Paul testifies that it isn't. When he was in trouble, this church had come to his aid, and he was very thankful. He knew what it was to be in need and had learned contentment from his own trials. His hadn't been an easy path. It takes strength, he admits, but he faced the trials through God, and he became an example to this young church.

Anyone who follows Paul's demanding truths will ultimately have a prosperous life of faith. The apostle promises: "Those things that you have both learned and received, and heard and seen in me, do, and the God of peace shall be with you" (Philippians 4:9).

Paul's prescription for the Philippians works for us too. Will we use it? There is nothing we cannot accomplish for God if we look to Him for strength and follow His will.

I can do all things through Christ who strengthens me.
PHILIPPIANS 4:13

49. RULES OR LOVE?

But those who wait on the LORD shall renew their strength. They shall mount up with wings like eagles, they shall run and not be weary, and they shall walk and not faint.

ISAIAH 40:31

The *buts* of scripture often indicate that something better is coming (or in this case has come). It's not like the excuse from your friend, "I'd like to help you next weekend, but I have something really important going on." God doesn't have anything more important in hand than loving you. And He proved it by sending Jesus to die for your sins to bring you into relationship with Him—a relationship that, unlike the law, didn't require constant sacrifices.

God gave His law to show mankind about Himself. The law showed people that He was holy, and people were not. But the law only offered a temporary solution. Animal sacrifices couldn't solve the sin problem—they only covered it for a short time.

All along, God had a better idea: Jesus. He is the *but* in John 1:17–18: "For the law was given by Moses, but grace and truth came by Jesus Christ. No man has seen God at any time. The only begotten Son, who is in the bosom of the Father, He has declared Him."

Through Christ, we have a perfect view of God Himself. Jesus told sinners that God wanted a relationship of grace and truth with them. And He was there to make that happen, just as had been promised in the law and the prophets.

Sometimes we get caught up in following rules. Of course, it *is* important that we know what God calls us to do or avoid. How can we please Him if we are ignorant of what He asks of us? But that's not the heart of knowing God. Faith in Jesus is. Why? Because God wants a loving relationship with His children.

Are you caught up in rules or love? The *buts* of scripture promised the better way.

But now in Christ Jesus you who sometimes were
far off are made near by the blood of Christ.
Ephesians 2:13

50. THOSE WHO. . .SHALL

*But those who wait on the LORD **shall** renew their strength.*
They shall mount up with wings like eagles, they shall run
and not be weary, and they shall walk and not faint.

ISAIAH 40:31

Isaiah 40:31 makes a promise to everyone who waits on the Lord. "Those who" do that "shall" be rewarded—with renewed strength, eagles' wings, the ability to walk and run without weariness.

Several other "those who. . .shall" promises appear in the psalms. Some are like Isaiah 40:31, offering encouragement to those of us who follow God. Others are warnings to those who don't serve and honor the Lord.

Though the latter seem negative, they're actually good news for good people: evildoers will get what their bad deeds deserve. For those who speak lies, "You [God] shall destroy" them (Psalm 5:6). "Those who are far from [God] shall perish" (Psalm 73:27). David wrote, in words that apply to all of God's beloved children, "Those who seek my soul to destroy it shall go into the lower parts of the earth" (Psalm 63:9).

But God's own people can claim the positive promises of several "those who. . .shall" scriptures:

- "Those who seek Him shall praise the LORD. Your heart shall live forever" (Psalm 22:26).

- "The LORD redeems the soul of His servants, and none of those who trust in Him shall be desolate" (Psalm 34:22).

- "For evildoers shall be cut off, but those who wait on the LORD, they shall inherit the earth" (Psalm 37:9).

- "Those who sow in tears shall reap in joy" (Psalm 126:5).

God is the ultimate authority. When He says something "shall" happen, it will. He is not a man, that He should lie (Numbers 24:19), and in fact, He cannot lie (Titus 1:2). You can be sure that if you are one of "those who," you "shall" receive whatever He promises.

Those who are planted in the house of the LORD shall flourish in the courts of our God.

PSALM 92:13

51. AVOID STUMBLING

But those who wait on the LORD shall renew their strength.
*They shall mount up with wings like eagles, they shall **run***
and not be weary, and they shall walk and not faint.

ISAIAH 40:31

Proverbs 4:11–12 includes the words of a father passing along wisdom to his son. It says, "I have taught you in the way of wisdom; I have led you in right paths. When you go, your steps shall not be hindered, and when you run, you shall not stumble."

Fathers often give advice to their children but wonder if they have wasted their breath. Will their children hear and follow, or do they have to learn every lesson all over again because they simply will not believe? No father wants to see his children make the same mistakes he made.

Wisdom leads us to better paths. Instead of walking smack into the middle of a dangerous swamp, we can jog down wisdom's pleasant, smooth path. Fathers, with their experience of life, know where the pitfalls are and try to point out the better way.

We want the best for our children, and so does our heavenly Father. God doesn't enjoy watching us fall into the traps of sin. But we'll stumble into them if we don't have wisdom to guide us.

Wise dads help their children understand the Bible. Throughout its pages are the ways of wisdom—knowledge greater than anything even the best earthly father could ever offer. Scripture contains the truth of a God who sees the future and knows our past. He knows everything about us, from what we think and do to how we are made (Psalm 139:2–3, 13–14).

The wisdom of the Bible isn't only for children. Scripture provides a lifelong walkway for believers of all ages. As we travel on the right paths, when we intimately know God's Word, we have the best guidance available. With it, we can run without stumbling.

As for God, His way is perfect. The word of the LORD is tried. He is a shield to all those who trust in Him.
PSALM 18:30

52. DO NOT REPAY

*But those who **wait** on the LORD shall renew their strength.*
They shall mount up with wings like eagles, they shall run
and not be weary, and they shall walk and not faint.

ISAIAH 40:31

When we see evil, especially in our own vicinity, it's hard to stand back and do nothing. But how many times have we rushed in to correct a wrong and found that we only made things worse?

Is there a wrong in your life? God knows about it, even if He hasn't solved the problem yet. Is there an injustice in the world? It will be corrected in eternity, even if it isn't made right on earth. Whatever evil is committed will be repaid because our Lord is the God of justice. He cannot let wrongdoing stand.

When we try to correct things in our own power, when we take people and situations into our own fallible hands, we cannot create the kind of justice God provides. Though He often takes longer than we think He should, He repays completely and correctly, accounting for every detail that fed into a particular situation.

World War II was a horrible event in world history. As the conflict dragged on, the people of England wondered if the fighting would end before they were destroyed—and Adolf Hitler did have a plan to invade England and set up a German puppet government. But through seemingly miraculous means, God brought about an Allied victory, stopping the evils of Hitler's Germany. Millions of lives had been lost and countless others changed forever. Perfect justice would be delayed until eternity, but from the ashes of war, God brought forth a reestablished state of Israel, as was prophesied in the Old Testament (Isaiah 11:12).

It is not our prerogative to repay evil. Instead, we should put everything in God's hands. We'll be amazed at the salvation He brings when we wait for Him.

Do not say, "I will repay evil," but wait
on the LORD, and He shall save you.
PROVERBS 20:22

53. BUT IF NOT. . .

***But** those who wait on the LORD shall renew their strength. They shall mount up with wings like eagles, they shall run and not be weary, and they shall walk and not faint.*

ISAIAH 40:31

Since Isaiah 40:31 begins with the word *but*, there's a contrast to what went before. And that was the statement that even young men and youths grow weary and faint apart from God's strength.

Some young men of Israel's history waited on God, using the little word *but* to indicate their trust in Him. Perhaps you remember the story of Shadrach, Meshach, and Abed-nego, refusing to bow to the Babylonian king Nebuchadnezzar's massive golden statue. Threatened with the "fiery furnace" as a punishment for their disobedience, they told the king, "If it be so, our God whom we serve is able to deliver us from the burning fiery furnace. And He will deliver us out of your hand, O king. *But* if not, let it be known to you, O king, that we will not serve your gods, nor worship the golden statue that you have set up" (Daniel 3:17–18, emphasis added).

These faithful men knew that God had the power to save them from the flames—from any punishment Nebuchadnezzar might try to impose. Even more, they believed that God *would* deliver them.

Still, Shadrach, Meshach, and Abed-nego allowed for the possibility that God would say no. . .and their *but* indicated they would still trust that God. There would be no bowing to a pagan king's statue.

We who follow God by faith in His Son, Jesus Christ, know that He provides the *but* to every human challenge. I'm weary, but He provides strength. The world is dangerous, but He delivers—either here on earth or in heaven to come. Life is tough, but He is much stronger, wiser, and better than any other resource we could try to imagine.

But can be misused: "*But* Lord, I don't want to!" *But* can also point us to the amazing benefits our Lord provides. Let's be sure to use the word in its most positive and beneficial way.

But now the righteousness of God without the law is clearly revealed by the deeds of the law, being witnessed by the Law and the Prophets, even the righteousness of God that is by faith in Jesus Christ, to all and on all those who believe.

ROMANS 3:21–22

54. STATE OF REALITY

But those who wait on the LORD shall renew their strength.
They shall mount up with wings like eagles, they shall run
*and not **be** weary, and they shall walk and not faint.*

ISAIAH 40:31

One of the shortest words in the English language carries some of the largest implications. The verb *be* has many definitions, but one of the most profound is this: "to have an objective existence; have reality or actuality."

Isaiah 40:31 uses the little verb to show that the actuality of weariness is counteracted by the renewed strength that God provides as we wait on Him. When we quiet our souls before God, when we spend time reading and contemplating His Word, when we talk to Him in prayer and listen for His voice in return, we're "waiting" on Him. And then He changes our reality, from "being weary" to "renewing our strength." We find those "wings like eagles," and we're able to walk and run without stumbling.

God is able to change our reality because He is the ultimate reality. Nothing exists apart from Him. He predated everything we see, know, and experience by the measure of eternity past. It's interesting to note that God's own name for Himself—I AM

(Exodus 3:14)—includes a form of the verb *be*. God described Himself as existing, and always in the present tense. . .there has never been a time that He wasn't, and there will never be a time that He isn't.

That is the state of reality as it concerns God. And He will carry those of us who love and follow Jesus through eternity future with a perfectly powerful existence like His own.

For now, though, in our aging, decaying bodies, we depend on the Lord day by day for strength. If you're feeling weary, look to God for strength and eagles' wings. He's waiting for you to wait on Him.

So Christ was sacrificed once to take away the sins of
many; and he will appear a second time, not to bear sin,
but to bring salvation to those who are waiting for him.
HEBREWS 9:28 NIV

55. ASK NOW

But those who wait on the LORD shall renew their strength.
They shall mount up with wings like eagles, they shall run
*and not be **weary**, and they shall walk and not faint.*

ISAIAH 40:31

Can you imagine never being weary, though you had all creation to oversee? How much energy would that require? What would it be like to go nonstop without tiring? Just thinking of it makes some of us want to take a nap.

Of course, being human, we will never have the strength or understanding to rule all of creation. And we wouldn't really want a job with such infinite demands. Isn't it comforting to know that God never gets weary, that He doesn't fall asleep at the wheel or have any limit to His power? He never misses a detail about the universe. He is perfectly capable of handling every need.

Our limited strength can never compare to God's. Our minds balk at trying to understand all that He is and does. Rather than trying to usurp His role, let's praise and worship Him for His awesomeness.

Life without God is simply a shadow of what it could be.

He wants to increase our strength and stamina, and He wants to do that generously.

Do you ever get weary? Feel as if you're fainting? Turn to Jesus, who is ready and willing to give you the power you're missing. When your strength is down to nothing, His never is. If you're weary, ask for help.

Have you not known? Have you not heard that the everlasting God, the LORD, the Creator of the ends of the earth, does not lose strength, nor is weary? There is no searching of His understanding. He gives power to the faint, and He increases the strength of those who have no might.
ISAIAH 40:28–29

56. DEEP-SIN DIVING

But those who wait on the LORD shall renew their strength.
They shall mount up with wings like eagles, they shall run
*and not be weary, and they shall walk and not **faint**.*

ISAIAH 40:31

Sometimes we feel faint from working so hard. But sometimes our weakness grows out of disobedience and folly.

The latter was the experience of the wayward prophet Jonah. Most everyone knows he was swallowed by a giant fish. Sunday school veterans know Jonah had been tossed into the water by pagan sailors, terrified of the wild storm that God sent against His prophet, who was running away from a command to preach to the violent city of Nineveh. Though they didn't want to do it, the sailors ultimately took Jonah's suggestion to throw him into the sea.

"I went down to the bottoms of the mountains; the earth with her bars was around me forever," Jonah recalled later. "Yet You have brought up my life from corruption, O LORD my God. When my soul fainted within me, I remembered the LORD, and my prayer came in to You, into Your holy temple" (Jonah 2:6–7).

Any sin in our lives causes trouble. Maybe not quite as

dramatic as Jonah's, but maybe so. When we allow ourselves to live in disobedience to God, it's not long before we know we need rescuing.

When our souls faint with fear or the knowledge that we never should have come to a certain place, we still have a source of help. God is willing to save us, as He was willing to save Jonah. While our breath bubbles up through the waters of sin and our lungs become empty of air, our hearts can still cry out to God. He is as close as a prayer.

Naturally, it's better if we never allow ourselves to be over-whelmed by sin. We shouldn't go deep-sin diving to give God a chance to rescue us. But even if we knowingly disobey Him, even if our soul is fainting due to our own folly, God doesn't give up on us. Yes, there may still be consequences—but God never withholds His love and forgiveness when we turn to Him (1 John 1:9).

No temptation has taken you but such as is common to man. But God is faithful, who will not allow you to be tempted above what you are able, but with the temptation will also make a way of escape, that you may be able to bear it.
1 Corinthians 10:13

57. STRENGTH AND GLADNESS

*But those who wait on the LORD shall renew their **strength**.*
They shall mount up with wings like eagles, they shall run
and not be weary, and they shall walk and not faint.
ISAIAH 40:31

Idolatry surrounds us, just as it did the ancient Israelites. We may not see wood, stone, or gold statues that portray a false deity, but we see plenty of people worshipping money, fame, sex, cars, or other created things. And we hear people denying God and His truth every day.

The most important things in our lives are what we worship. Like ancient peoples, humans today may worship more than one "god." Even good things can become gods if we let them get out of balance in our lives. Anything that does not bring glory to God can distract us from Him.

That's why He commanded, "You shall have no other gods before me" (Exodus 20:3). And the wording doesn't imply that we can have another god on the side, in addition to our Lord. "You shall worship no other god," He said, "for the LORD, whose name is Jealous, is a jealous God" (Exodus 34:14). Our God wants us to worship Him and Him alone. Just as an honorable man doesn't have his wife and another woman on the side, God is a single commitment.

But why would anyone *want* any other god? He provides the strength we need for life. What more could we possibly need?

If you struggle with the temptation to overemphasize other things—a relationship, a possession, a habit—consciously remind yourself that God gives strength. He is all-powerful, and He wants to provide the power you need to live well. . .to live up to His standards.

You don't need any other god when you have Jesus. Give Him all the things that pull at your heart, and feel the strength He gives in return.

For all the gods of the people are idols, but the LORD made the heavens. Glory and honor are in His presence; strength and gladness are in His place. Give to the LORD, you families of the people, give to the LORD glory and strength.
1 CHRONICLES 16:26–28

58. LIKE SHEEP?

But those who wait on the LORD shall renew their strength.
*They shall mount up with wings **like** eagles, they shall run*
and not be weary, and they shall walk and not faint.

ISAIAH 40:31

Like is a comparison word that can go either way, one that's positive or not so complimentary.

Rising up on wings like eagles—who wouldn't want that in their spiritual life? Hopefully, we've all felt and enjoyed such a spiritual high at some point. But scripture doesn't tell us to live on a high; it's just not realistic.

Here's one of the downs, perhaps: being compared to a silly sheep. "We all like sheep have gone astray," the prophet Isaiah wrote. "We have turned, each one, to his own way" (53:6).

Maybe we enjoy the image of lambs romping in a field. But there's certainly a messier side of sheep. And, honestly, they're kind of dumb and prone to getting into trouble. Maybe we don't really appreciate God comparing us to these wooly creatures.

But God is always truthful. While we want to be "like eagles," we are often "like sheep." When we don't take the guidance of our Shepherd, we wander off into bad places. We can end up in terrible trouble.

Thankfully, God has many ways of redirecting us. We can read His Word and discover a passage that seems as if it was meant for us. (Actually, before time began, God knew what that passage would mean to you.) A wise friend may offer advice. Or some unexpected benefit may fall into our laps, and we recognize it as God's provision. Sometimes when we pray, we'll get a feeling that we're off track, and that sensation may be God's Spirit nudging us back in the right direction.

We'd rather be like eagles than sheep. But in our times of careless straying, we can be sure that God is watching us with His eagle eye, ready to pull His silly sheep out of trouble.

But let all those who put their trust in You rejoice.
Let them ever shout for joy because You defend them.
Let those also who love Your name be joyful in You.
Psalm 5:11

59. TRUST COMPLETELY

*But those who **wait** on the LORD shall renew their strength. They shall mount up with wings like eagles, they shall run and not be weary, and they shall walk and not faint.*

ISAIAH 40:31

When life turns desperate, we have a wonderful opportunity to trust in God. But will we?

The prophet Micah described a situation in which even his own household members had become enemies—and he was thrown into God's arms: "A man's enemies are the men of his own house. Therefore, I will look to the LORD. I will wait for the God of my salvation. My God will hear me" (7:6–7). When no one else could help, the Lord could intervene and relieve the prophet's uncomfortable condition (see Psalm 124:8).

Desperate situations are designed to make us wait for God. As long as we have another option, we may pursue it. Maybe we think God wants us to go as far as we can on our own before we turn to Him, and we subscribe to Benjamin Franklin's aphorism, "God helps those who help themselves." Nothing could be further from the truth. God doesn't expect us to wear ourselves out with other, failing methods when we can go straight to Him. But we often chase every other option first.

Why don't we rush to request God's help? Maybe it's because we know that He sometimes makes us wait, and that's uncomfortable. We'd prefer to have a quick resolution. If God doesn't jump to meet our schedule, we doubt if He will answer at all.

But when push comes to shove, and all our self-help solutions have failed, we realize that God is our best—really, our only—help. At that moment, we can heave our huge sack of troubles into our Savior's arms. And we can trust Him completely to deal with it, rather than snatching it back and trying something else.

Go to God with your needs, great and small, right from the beginning. Wait for Him. Trust Him, and He will answer at the right time.

God is our refuge and strength,
a very present help in trouble.
PSALM 46:1

60. IMMOVABLE, UNSHAKEABLE

But those who wait on the LORD shall renew their strength.
*They shall mount up with wings **like** eagles, they shall run*
and not be weary, and they shall walk and not faint.

ISAIAH 40:31

The Bible has delightful word pictures that help us understand spiritual truths. One of the methods scripture uses is to make comparisons.

If God simply told us, "My righteousness never changes," we'd get the idea. We know God is great. But when the psalm writer David says, "Your righteousness is like the great mountains" (Psalm 36:6), it hits not just our minds, but our hearts. We can visualize God's righteousness *and* His power. So when Malachi says, "I am the LORD; I do not change" (3:6), we have a picture of a mountain that never experiences so much as a rock slip.

When God compares Himself to earthly things, He tells us that He *is* a rock or fortress (Psalm 18:2) or a strong tower (Proverbs 18:10). And 1 Samuel 2:2 says, "There is no one holy like the LORD, for there is no one besides You, nor is there any rock like our God." He is not *like* the earthly things used in our word pictures because He is their creator. God doesn't get His strength from His creation—it's the other way around.

The word *like* may describe people, animals, or other objects, but as scripture repeatedly tells us, there is none like God (Exodus 8:10; 2 Samuel 7:22; Psalm 86:8). We may share a bit of His nature as we share His "likeness" (Genesis 5:1), but that is small potatoes compared to the totality of a holy Lord.

Like doesn't mean "the same as." When we get a picture in scripture, we need to be careful not to go too far with it. God's righteousness is similar to a mountain, but it is much greater. God Himself is the all-powerful Creator to whom all created things are compared. He is our immovable, unshakeable mountain. He is also our Father!

Your righteousness is like the great mountains;
Your judgments are a great deep. O LORD,
You preserve man and beast.
PSALM 36:6

61. WAITING WELL

*But those who **wait** on the LORD shall renew their strength.*
They shall mount up with wings like eagles, they shall run
and not be weary, and they shall walk and not faint.

ISAIAH 40:31

We don't often feel as if waiting is good. When we were children, we could barely sleep on Christmas Eve because we knew good things were coming the next day. As we grew up, we often wanted to speed things along, making our plans happen immediately. We have goals for our lives and a schedule for them. We need to get things done at work, in our family, at church. Waiting isn't a good thing as far as men are concerned.

But Isaiah 40:31 isn't about getting a Christmas present or even completing a job. We are looking at a heavenly situation with God in charge of what's happening. A delay on a work project might get us in trouble with the boss or a client. But God's timing is different. He is dealing with eternal issues—the soul of every person on earth. And if that takes a while from our perspective, so be it. God is beyond deadlines, time, and our human limitations.

Salvation comes to us in many ways. It begins when we

accept Christ and receive forgiveness from sin and a place in God's kingdom. But God doesn't stop there. Throughout our lives, He is saving us from sinful errors and keeping us from harm. And, as we see in Isaiah 40:31, He saves us from our own weakness.

Times of waiting will come, and that's okay. We are no longer children longing for Christmas morning, so we need not worry when life doesn't unfold exactly as we might wish. We know that God has whatever we're waiting for well under His control. And we know that, if we love and obey Him, all things will work out to our good (Romans 8:28).

It is good that a man should both hope and
quietly wait for the salvation of the LORD.
LAMENTATIONS 3:26

62. WHAT COMES FIRST?

But those who wait on the LORD shall renew their strength.
They shall mount up with wings like eagles, they shall run
and not be weary, and they shall walk and not faint.

ISAIAH 40:31

When applied to God, the title *Lord* means He has power and authority over all. Giving God control of our lives in spiritual matters may not seem difficult, but for some people, the idea that their earnings and physical possessions are also due to Him seems a bit much. Putting a few dollars in the plate on Sunday is fine, but a tithe? Ten percent? *Does God really need that much?* some may ask.

God doesn't usually ask for all our possessions, though it is within His right as Lord of heaven and earth. Nothing we receive comes to us apart from Him.

Much of what He gives us, though, He gives so we can honor Him by sharing with others. We may open our homes to a Bible study group and honor God that way, or we may give to our church regularly, adding extra donations in times of need. But the greatest challenge may be generously giving to God without expectation of return. And God does expect us to share our best, our "firstfruits." That can be a challenging spiritual demand because not giving willingly shows our lack of trust in God or the greed that fills our hearts.

We tend to cling to our physical possessions because they represent security. Money in the bank means safety on a rainy day. A home is a shelter. A car is a means to freedom. We can become wrapped up in these things.

God warns us against security in earthly possessions: "Do not lay up for yourselves treasures on earth, where moth and rust corrupt, and where thieves break in and steal," and follows it with a promise, "But lay up for yourselves treasures in heaven, where neither moth nor rust corrupts, and where thieves do not break in or steal" (Matthew 6:19–20).

The way we handle physical things shows where our sense of security lies. Are we trusting in a nice home to shelter us—or God? What comes first?

Honor the LORD with your possessions and
with the firstfruits of all your increase.
PROVERBS 3:9

63. LASTING RENEWAL

*But those who wait on the LORD shall **renew** their strength.*
They shall mount up with wings like eagles, they shall run
and not be weary, and they shall walk and not faint.

ISAIAH 40:31

Psalm 103 tells us not to forget God's many benefits, including His provision of food. God's generosity renews our youth like the eagle's (verse 5). Does that sound similar to those who were waiting for their strength to be renewed in Isaiah 40? Surely it's no coincidence.

Renewing can actually be hard, intense work. But the verses in Psalm 103 remind us of God's benefits to those who seemingly have done nothing to earn it. In fact, this entire psalm speaks of God's benefits: His love, forgiveness, and mercy to frail humans. None of those can be earned; they are freely given by a loving God, who gives them as gifts.

When we are satisfied with good food, even if we worked to get the money to pay for it, we need to be reminded that it too comes from God, who provides the rain for crops and the grass, hay, and corn that feed the animals we feast on. And when we eat and feel our strength returning to us, we need to remember who is renewing our strength.

But greater than all the physical needs God provides for are our spiritual ones. Most of Psalm 103 doesn't focus on the physical benefits of knowing God because they are surpassed by all His spiritual blessings. He has given us spiritual renewal through His forgiveness, mercy, righteous judgment, and loving-kindness.

We can and should rightly thank God for the physical renewal we get through food. But let's not forget to thank Him also for the many methods of spiritual renewal He has brought into our lives through the salvation offered by Jesus. The strength from a meal may last for a few hours, but spiritual renewal is available for eternity.

And God said, "Behold, I have given you every herb-bearing seed that is on the face of all the earth and every tree, in which is the fruit of a tree-yielding seed; to you it shall be for food."
GENESIS 1:29

64. DISCOURAGEMENT SLOWDOWN

*But those who wait on the LORD shall renew their **strength**.
They shall mount up with wings like eagles, they shall run
and not be weary, and they shall walk and not faint.*

ISAIAH 40:31

After they had been exiled to Babylon, God sent some Jews home. But when they arrived, they found their capital city in great disrepair, and discouragement filled them. Later, Nehemiah, cupbearer to Persian king Artaxerxes, heard of their troubles and shared that information with the king, who sent him to Jerusalem to help.

When he arrived, Nehemiah encouraged the people of Jerusalem to rebuild the city walls. They were heartened by the news that the king supported their efforts, and Nehemiah reminded them of the goodness of God. After that, Nehemiah 2:18 says, "So they strengthened their hands for this good work."

Sometimes all a weakened believer needs is a few words of encouragement to be strengthened. When he knows all is not lost and God hasn't given up on him, his heart lifts, and he readies himself for more of God's work. And several encouraged people can start to support each other in faith and work together to make the work lighter. Nehemiah broke up the responsibilities for the rebuilding, so each family had its own responsibility, and the work moved forward rapidly.

Everyone experiences slowdowns from discouragement. But a good leader or friend can speak words that fuel renewed action. Sometimes those words don't have to be well-spoken. A simple reminder of the truths of God's Word can be enough. Listeners may have known the truths for many years, but "a word spoken in due season—how good is it!" (Proverbs 15:23).

Alone, we may allow discouragement to make our feet stick to the floor, but the kind words of another can get us going again. Is there someone you know who is feeling a little blue today? Strengthen him by picking up the phone or sending a text to let him know he's not alone.

---

*Therefore, comfort one another and edify
one another, even as you also are doing.*
1 THESSALONIANS 5:11

65. GROANING FOR HOME

But those who wait on the LORD shall renew their strength.
They shall mount up with wings like eagles, they shall run
*and not be weary, and they shall **walk** and not faint.*

ISAIAH 40:31

Though we may seem quite at home in our bodies, we are just walking in them for a time. Like everything on earth, they do not last forever. Illness comes, and eventually we have to roll up our earthly tent and head for our heavenly home, "a building from God, a house not made with hands, eternal in the heavens" (2 Corinthians 5:1).

In the meantime, we live in our tents, always thinking of the day when we will move into that heavenly house. Paul says we groan to be clothed with our heavenly home (Romans 8:23). As we walk by faith in this land, our desire to be with God grows. And we become ever more grateful for the eternal life that Jesus provides.

The longer we live in this world, the more trouble and sorrow we see. The walk of this life begins to make us weary and faint—which necessitates our waiting on God. We wait for Him to strengthen us for the obligations of this world, but we also wait on Him for the ultimate renewal of all things, when the entire universe is gladly serving Jesus Christ as King.

Nonbelievers, who can't understand why we live our lives so differently, may choose to mock our walk. But we can remain confident in the heavenly things we have yet to see. The deposit of the Spirit in our hearts guarantees that God has more for us after this life (2 Corinthians 5:5).

Because we love God, though we have yet to see all He has for us, we walk in ways that please Him. And we trust that in eternity we will see the results of our faith. We can be as sure of that as we are of everything we see here on earth.

---

*As you have therefore received Christ Jesus the
Lord, so walk in Him, rooted and built up in
Him, and established in the faith, as you have been
taught, abounding in it with thanksgiving.*
COLOSSIANS 2:6–7

66. WHO ARE THOSE PEOPLE?

*But **those** who wait on the LORD shall renew their strength.*
They shall mount up with wings like eagles, they shall run
and not be weary, and they shall walk and not faint.

ISAIAH 40:31

Did you know that *those* is a pronoun? It's actually the plural of *that*, a word defined as "one of the indicated kind." In Isaiah 40:31, *those*—as a pronoun—stands in for a class of people, the ones who wait on the Lord.

That's a good group to be part of. It's better than any human family. It's better than any club or organization. It's even better than any church, since not everyone in every church is waiting on God. If you're one of those who do wait on God, you'll find that His renewing of strength makes every other relationship better.

And there are several other groups of "those people" blessed by God. Consider just a few examples:

- "Blessed are all those who put their trust in Him" (Psalm 2:12).

- "And those who know Your name will put their trust in You, for You, Lord, have not forsaken those who seek You" (Psalm 9:10).

- "As for God, His way is perfect. The word of the Lord is tried. He is a shield to all those who trust in Him" (Psalm 18:30).

- "All the paths of the Lord are mercy and truth to those who keep His covenant and His testimonies" (Psalm 25:10).

- "Oh how great is Your goodness, which You have laid up for those who fear You, which You have worked for those who trust in You before the sons of men!" (Psalm 31:19).

- "Behold, the eye of the Lord is on those who fear Him, on those who hope in His mercy, to deliver their soul from death and to keep them alive in famine" (Psalm 33:18–19).

- "The angel of the Lord encamps around those who fear him and delivers them" (Psalm 34:7).

- "The Lord is near to those who have of a broken heart and saves those who have a contrite spirit" (Psalm 34:18).

Aspire to be one of "those people."

The Lord will give grace and glory; no good thing will He withhold from those who walk uprightly.
PSALM 84:11

67. NO FEAR

But those who wait on the LORD shall renew their strength. They shall mount up with wings like eagles, they shall run and not be weary, and they shall walk and not faint.

ISAIAH 40:31

Isaiah 40:31 is an optimistic, positive verse. But it's built on the negative ideas of weakness, weariness, and even fear—of our human incapability.

Fear is really man's natural state. When Satan controls a life, there is much to fear. Without God's love and protection, the world is a harsh, demanding place, and people have no ability to soften it or even successfully think their way through all the ills of this world. The world without Jesus is empty and dangerous.

But when we come to Christ, we gain access to so much that the natural man cannot have. God gives us the power to live in Him, and love fills our lives. Our minds become clear under the rule of God's Word, and the Spirit fills our hearts and minds. We can live in the alternative world of "power and of love and of a sound mind" (2 Timothy 1:7).

That's not to say that Christians never fear. The natural world tugs at our hearts in many ways. *But* as believers, we have options other than sin.

Paul exhorted young Timothy to live in the faith he had learned from his family. Timothy's belief was sincere, and the apostle had laid hands on him so he could work as a leader. But the commitment Timothy made on that day didn't end with one uplifting experience, any more than we can come to Christ in joy, then allow ourselves to slip into fearful living. Paul called on his follower to "stir up the gift of God" that was in him and not to be timid (2 Timothy 1:5–7).

To live in God's power and love and with a sound mind, we too must stir up whatever gift He has given us. It may not be one of leadership, like Timothy's, but if we live soundly in His love and power, we too can testify to God's greatness and share His love with the world.

"Have I not commanded you? Be strong and of good courage. Do not be afraid or be dismayed, for the LORD your God is with you wherever you go."

JOSHUA 1:9

68. SCRATCH THE SURFACE?

*But those who wait on the LORD shall **renew** their strength.*
They shall mount up with wings like eagles, they shall run
and not be weary, and they shall walk and not faint.

ISAIAH 40:31

From Paul and his coworkers, the Ephesians had heard the truth about Jesus. But they had not learned the truths of Christ to the point where they were willing to make a break with the sinful society around them. So the apostle admonished them to put off the sins of the pagan people around them, "who, being past feeling, have given themselves over to lewdness, to work all uncleanness with greediness" (Ephesians 4:19).

Hearing about and being taught by Jesus are good things. But they don't mean much if we never put those truths into action. Saying you are a Christian and showing it are two sides of one coin. You can't have one without the other. If you do, perhaps the commitment didn't go further than a scratch on the coin's surface.

For the Ephesians, who lived in an important, cosmopolitan trading city, the temptations of the world were constantly in front of them—and behind them and to each side too. The idea of standing out in their community for having faith was challenging. Some members of their community were not happy with this faith that excluded paganism.

But the apostle encouraged these new Christians to put off the "deceitful lusts" (Ephesians 4:22) of their old life and to let their new minds in Christ take control of a renewal that would bring a better life of righteousness and holiness.

Renewal of anything is challenging. But the renewal of our minds and hearts through Jesus Christ brings eternally satisfying results. Will we merely scratch the surface or go deeper today?

And He who sat on the throne said,
"Behold, I make all things new."
REVELATION 21:5

69. LORD OF ALL

But those who wait on the LORD shall renew their strength.
They shall mount up with wings like eagles, they shall run
and not be weary, and they shall walk and not faint.

ISAIAH 40:31

To be renewed in our strength, we can't wait on just anyone. Your wife or a friend or a business associate can't renew your strength in the way that "the Lord" does. That's because "the Lord" is God—all powerful, all knowing, absolutely unique.

There is a story about an evangelist and his friend in the days shortly after the American Revolution. Near Philadelphia, the heart of the new nation so recently freed from British control, they found a sign reading, "We serve no king here." Dismayed, the evangelist wondered how he could preach Jesus as King to a people who clearly wanted no part of any king. Not only in the United States but throughout the world, human beings value freedom. Many of us don't want to be told what to do and bristle at the thought of subservience. But then we come face-to-face with Jesus and His claim to be Lord.

Do we recognize what we're saying when we claim His name and use the word *Lord*? It actually means "all that I am and all that I possess I yield to You."

Jesus knows whether we're just paying lip service. To truly call Him "Lord" is to honestly, sincerely, earnestly—now and forever—give Jesus our entire lives. If we're holding anything back from Him, He'll know it. He wants all we are and all we value, treasure, and possess.

The truth is, none of those things are ours anyway. Everything is His. He has simply entrusted our lives, talents, and possessions to our stewardship. If and when He commands us to give something up, He has that right. But He also gives us the freedom to say no.

But why would we want to say no? He is the Lord who renews and strengthens us, the God who loves us to the point of self-sacrifice. Let's make Him truly the Lord of all in our lives.

---

*"You call Me Master and Lord, and you
are right to say it, for so I am."*
JOHN 13:13

70. EXPECTATION

*But those who **wait** on the LORD shall renew their strength.*
They shall mount up with wings like eagles, they shall run
and not be weary, and they shall walk and not faint.

ISAIAH 40:31

Is there someone you expect help from? Maybe your brother-in-law promised to help you move, or someone from your church agreed to lead a Bible study when you asked him. Perhaps they will come through for you, impressively. Or maybe situations beyond their control will intervene. Your brother-in-law could hurt his back, or a job commitment may crash the idea of the church leader taking on another commitment. Even the most well-meaning and consistent people can end up not being able to help. You may wait for them in vain.

Help doesn't always come when we expect it or in the way we figured it would. But no matter how long we have to wait, we know that even if our friend, family, or church cannot do it, God will always come through for us. And the Bible describes His help as "salvation," not just a day or a few weeks of offering a helping hand. His aid is complete.

As long as they're within His will, you can never have

expectations from God that are not fulfilled. You may not get an inheritance that makes you wealthy, but He will provide for you daily, just as He provides for the lilies of the field.

Our hope in God doesn't last a short time but throughout our lives. No matter how young or old we are, we need not feel discouraged or doubtful. We look to Him with a sense of expectation for many good things that lie before us, confident that no trouble deters Him. Our waiting will not be pointless; our difficulties will not lie beyond His aid.

Trust in Him for your salvation, no matter what you need. Who else could be your immovable Rock?

Truly my soul waits for God; from Him comes my
salvation. He alone is my rock and my salvation.
He is my defense; I shall not be greatly moved.
PSALM 62:1–2

71. TURN IT AROUND

But those who wait on the LORD shall renew their strength.
They shall mount up with wings like eagles, they shall run
*and **not** be weary, and they shall walk and not faint.*

ISAIAH 40:31

Not is considered a "function word," one that makes a negative or turns an idea around. In Isaiah 40:31, *not* negates our human weariness and fainting, due to our waiting on a strong and gracious Lord.

Once we've waited on God and received His strength, we can accomplish all kinds of good things—and negate many bad ones. Consider these examples from the Psalms:

- "I will not be afraid of ten thousands of people who have set themselves against me all around" (Psalm 3:6).

- "The sorrows of those who hurry after another god shall be multiplied. I will not offer their drink offerings of blood or take up their names on my lips" (Psalm 16:4).

- "For I will not trust in my bow, nor shall my sword save me. But You have saved us from our enemies and have put those who hated us to shame" (Psalm 44:6–7).

- "In God (I will praise His word), in God I have put my trust; I will not fear what flesh can do to me" (Psalm 56:4).

- "In God (I will praise His word), in the LORD (I will praise His word), in God I have put my trust; I will not be afraid of what man can do to me" (Psalm 56:10–11).

- "I will cut off whoever secretly slanders his neighbor. I will not endure him who has a haughty look and a proud heart" (Psalm 101:5).

- "The LORD is on my side; I will not fear. What can man do to me?" (Psalm 118:6).

- "I will delight myself in Your statutes. I will not forget Your word" (Psalm 119:16).

Want to live a positive, healthy, product life spiritually? Turn it around with a well-placed *not*. And if you need help with that, just ask God. He'll be happy to help.

Yes, though I walk through the valley of the shadow of death, I will not fear evil, for You are with me.
PSALM 23:4

72. A CHOICE

But those who wait on the LORD shall renew their strength.
They shall mount up with wings like eagles, they shall run
and not be weary, and they shall walk and not faint.

ISAIAH 40:31

Many who don't know Jesus would like to deny that He is Lord and God. They express reasons He couldn't be, but most of these ultimately come down to the fact that they want to live under their own power. They like life the way it is and may have opted to live that way without knowing they're under the command of Satan. They have missed a better choice.

Scripture describes two options and forces us to make a decision between living for God or going against Him in rebellion. Psalm 1 compares those two options: being a believing man who "shall be like a tree planted by the rivers of water that brings forth its fruit in its season. His leaf also shall not wither, and whatever he does shall prosper" (verse 3) or the rebel "like the chaff that the wind drives away" who "shall not stand in the judgment" (verses 4–5).

Sin makes us want to run our own lives, live our own way. We like to feel like we are in control and may believe we are—until we realize nothing could be less true. Living under Satan's rule leads to spiritual emptiness and death. That's the price of sin. But if we insist on making that choice, God will let us.

Or we can accept the sacrifice of Jesus as Lord, submitting to Him and living like the prosperous tree that drinks in the blessings of God on earth. And better than a tree, we then receive eternal life with Him.

Everyone must make the decision: Who will be my Lord? Because one way or another, each of us serves someone: Satan or God. There are no other options.

Death or life? What have you chosen? And whom will you live for now?

For the wages of sin is death, but the gift of God
is eternal life through Jesus Christ our Lord.
Romans 6:23

73. RUNNING FROM GOD

*But those who wait on the LORD shall renew their strength. They shall mount up with wings like eagles, they shall **run** and not be weary, and they shall walk and not faint.*

ISAIAH 40:31

No one should ever run in the direction of the evil described in Isaiah 59, which pictures the separation between God and His people: "Their feet run to evil, and they hurry to shed innocent blood. Their thoughts are thoughts of iniquity; devastation and destruction are in their paths" (verse 7). If there was ever a way not to run, this is it.

As God began to judge these sinners, they blindly wondered if His arm was too short to save them (verse 1). Perhaps they'd been influenced by the pagan ideas of the people around them, whose gods certainly had nothing but short wooden or metal arms. But Judah's people certainly hadn't been listening to their own prophets, who had tried to help them avoid sin.

Instead they had persistently sinned. "Your iniquities have separated you from your God, and your sins have hidden His face from you so that He will not hear," declared God to His doubting people. And He continued, "Your lips have spoken lies, your tongue has muttered perverseness. No one calls for justice; no one pleads for truth. They trust in vanity and speak lies. They conceive evil and produce iniquity" (verses 2–4).

They were headed for destruction. Though they ran toward the edge of a cliff, they didn't have a clue. Nothing Isaiah said deterred them, and no one seemed to turn to God for help. So God saved them by a drastic method, sending them into exile in Babylon.

Have you been running away from God? Turn back before it is too late. He may not send you to a distant country because you have headed in the wrong direction, but it's in your interest to have Him painfully intervene in your life. He loves you too much not to do so.

"If My people who are called by My name shall humble themselves and pray and seek My face and turn from their wicked ways, then I will hear from heaven and will forgive their sin and will heal their land."

2 CHRONICLES 7:14

74. WISE OR FOOLISH?

But those who wait on the LORD shall renew their strength.
They shall mount up with wings like eagles, they shall run
and not be weary, and they shall walk and not faint.

ISAIAH 40:31

Some people claim Jesus as Lord, but you'd never know it by their lifestyle. They'll say they are Christians, but when you read the Bible, you don't see their choices reflected in the Word.

God doesn't set us up as judges, and we don't have full knowledge of anyone's spiritual state—but we can get an idea of others' faith by looking at their fruit. A "Christian" who doesn't spend much time in the church, approves of attitudes that are not biblical, and doesn't do much good for others lacks good fruit.

That doesn't mean we get to decide if another man will make it to heaven. If he repents, he may well be with Jesus in eternity, and we should pray he will do just that. Only God gets to decide who enters heaven and who doesn't. Jesus simply admonished us to treat others as we would like to be treated, not see to it that they toe the line (Matthew 7:12). But "every good tree brings forth good fruit" (Matthew 7:17). When we see those who claim the lordship of Christ and don't live it, we shouldn't follow them into spiritual disaster.

Each of us must decide if Jesus is his Lord. But to do that, we each need to know what that means. God expects a serious commitment when we claim His name and call him Lord, not just a nod of the head and a life that goes its own way.

Jesus calls people who do not take His authority seriously "foolish" (Matthew 7:26). They are heading for destruction. Only the wise hear and follow His commands.

Today are you being wise or foolish? If someone looked at your life, would he see your commitment to your Lord? If not, what do you need to change?

"Not everyone who says to Me, 'Lord, Lord,'
shall enter into the kingdom of heaven, but he
who does the will of my Father who is in heaven."
MATTHEW 7:21

75. ALL THE DIFFERENCE

*But those who wait on the LORD shall **renew** their strength.*
They shall mount up with wings like eagles, they shall run
and not be weary, and they shall walk and not faint.

ISAIAH 40:31

Our spiritual strength is not renewed by exercising, physical rest, or any earthly effort we may try. When we are spiritually worn out, we cannot bring ourselves into renewal by any of it. Only God's Spirit renews us, and apart from His work in our lives, we cannot mount up with eagles' wings.

Under our own power, God tells us, we cannot dredge up spiritual strength. Even if we grabbed on to an eagle, it wouldn't provide us with the ability to live holy lives. So God made a way where there was no way, through His Son's sacrifice.

Let's face it. Jesus didn't agree to save us because we were so wonderful. It's not as if He couldn't resist the opportunity to die a painful death on the cross. He chose to do that because it was God the Father's will, and the whole Godhead—Father, Son, and Spirit—filled with love and mercy, willingly chose to go to all the trouble that salvation would require.

God could have chosen to give up on mankind, but it wasn't

consistent with His nature. Love and mercy flow from Him, despite their terrible cost. So even when His children fail, He does not desert us.

God will not give up on you, so don't give up on Him. Instead remember all the love and kindness He has lavished on you through the sacrifice of His Son. Appreciate the mercy that has flooded your life as He washed you through regeneration and gave you renewal for your whole life.

Praise Him for the love, mercy, and forgiveness that has filled your life because of His nature. He renewed your life based on His love, not your actions, and it has made all the difference.

But after that the kindness and love of God our Savior toward man appeared, not by works of righteousness that we have done, but according to His mercy He saved us, by the washing of regeneration and renewing of the Holy Spirit.
TITUS 3:4–5

76. HIS WORKMANSHIP

But those who wait on the LORD shall renew their strength.
They shall mount up with wings like eagles, they shall run
and not be weary, and they shall walk and not faint.

ISAIAH 40:31

The *but* that begins Isaiah 40:31 sets obedient believers apart from other people. They are the ones who will renew their strength by waiting on God.

Obedience is an expectation of New Testament believers as well. When God saves us through Jesus Christ, He begins to fashion us into what He has destined us to become. He has prepared good works beforehand for us to walk in and accomplish (Ephesians 2:10) for the sake of His kingdom that is coming and that we make visible in the here and now (Matthew 5:13–16). These works do not save us, but they give clear evidence of our redemption and sanctification.

German philosopher Friedrich Nietzsche said, "I might believe in the Redeemer if his followers looked more redeemed." What Nietzsche said may be convicting. In Galatians 5:19–23 (emphasis added), we are shown a dichotomy between works of the flesh (our sin nature) and works of the Spirit: "Now the works of the flesh are evident, which are these: adultery, fornication, uncleanness, lewdness, idolatry, witchcraft, hatred, dissensions, jealousies, wrath, strife, rebellions, heresies, envyings, murders, drunkenness, immoral festivals, and similar. . . . *But* the fruit of the Spirit is love, joy, peace, long-suffering, gentleness, goodness, faith, meekness, self-control. Against such there is no law."

Before God saved us, we walked in the darkness of our fallenness as spiritually dead men. After He saves us, we still walk as fallen beings, *but* now the indwelling of the Holy Spirit causes us to bear fruit despite our fallenness. This fruit is a manifestation of divine influence and energy at work in us, leading us to be salt and light for our Lord in a broken world. This is our mission as we walk and run with the strength He gives us.

We will struggle against the effects of our fallenness until we draw our last breath. Though we fail, our Father who called us is faithful, providing everything we need to triumph and get back on His path. We need never resign ourselves to defeat.

Remember, the Nietzsches of the world are watching. Are we living after the *but* of Galatians or in the fleshly works that come before?

Grow in grace and in the knowledge of
our Lord and Savior Jesus Christ.
2 Peter 3:18

77. AWAITING CROPS

*But those who **wait** on the LORD shall renew their strength.*
They shall mount up with wings like eagles, they shall run
and not be weary, and they shall walk and not faint.

ISAIAH 40:31

The New Testament writer James compared waiting to a farmer holding off on harvesting his crop: "Be patient therefore, brothers, until the coming of the Lord. Behold, the farmer waits for the precious fruit of the earth and has long patience for it, until he receives the early and latter rain" (James 5:7).

In biblical Israel, the farmer planted barley and winter wheat in October or November and waited until April to June for the harvest. Early rains fed the seeds and seedlings, and the latter rains watered the grain nearing harvest.

Had the farmer tried to rush things, he would have destroyed his crop. Everyone in Israel knew that if you left your wheat or barley crop to grow, in the late spring or early summer you had a good crop if rains came at the proper time.

Waiting wasn't easy for farmers who risked their own lives on the crops they could bring in. A poor crop could mean very little bread and a lot of hunger for a family until the next harvest.

So when James encouraged us to wait, he wasn't saying it was easy. He knew the crops were the lifeline of a family. He knew that crop was precious to every family member, and they all would take part in working the fields to increase their success.

Just as a farmer must be patient and trust that the rains will water the crops so he can feed his family, we must wait for the return of our King. When life is tumultuous, we trust that God has something growing underneath the ground. Just as the farmer had to trust that the Lord would bring the rains, we must have faith that God is working out something for our good (Romans 8:28).

As the farmer knew his seeds would grow, we know our Lord will return. He has promised, and He will do it. Just be patient.

Behold, He comes with clouds,
and every eye shall see Him.
REVELATION 1:7

78. NO DESPAIR!

But those who wait on the LORD shall renew their strength. They shall mount up with wings like eagles, they shall run and not be weary, and they shall walk and not faint.

ISAIAH 40:31

Paul was a man who understood Isaiah 40:31. His ministry was challenging. He didn't get much time to sit by the fire and rest, and when he wasn't moving, he was probably in a nasty jail cell. Trouble seemed to follow him.

Paul had been stoned (Acts 14:19), beaten, jailed (Acts 16:23), and shipwrecked, even spending a night and day in the sea (2 Corinthians 11:25). So when he said, "We are troubled on every side," in 2 Corinthians 4:8, we believe him. It's not hard to understand he'd been perplexed, and we've seen the persecutions he went through in his story throughout the book of Acts. Life certainly seemed destined to keep him pinned down.

But none of this halted Paul. He knew how to wait on the Lord and find renewed strength. Trouble, despair, and sufferings couldn't stop Paul because his mission statement was always before him. Difficulties were his own way of bearing the death of Jesus, so others could envision the sacrifice our Lord had made for them.

It doesn't matter if we have physical or emotional distress that invades our lives. Whatever our discouragement, we—like Paul—should remember this life doesn't have the last say. Jesus does. As long as we are on this earth, we can testify to His love and grace, and Paul did that better through the hardships he endured.

Facing troubles? Don't despair. Paul sets the example of faithful, patient service—and success. Remember that Jesus' sufferings saved you, and He is making Himself evident in whatever you are going through.

Trust Him and experience the *but* that takes on discouragement and wins. Nothing can cause us to despair if we keep our eyes on Jesus.

---

*For I consider that the sufferings of this present
time are not worthy to be compared with
the glory that shall be revealed in us.*
ROMANS 8:18

79. WHOM SHOULD I FEAR?

But those who wait on the LORD shall renew their strength.
They shall mount up with wings like eagles, they shall run
and not be weary, and they shall walk and not faint.

ISAIAH 40:31

The night before his assassination, Dr. Martin Luther King Jr., while speaking to an audience that gathered to hear him, said, "I'm not afraid of any man." Centuries before, King David wrote, "The LORD is my light and my salvation. Whom shall I fear? The LORD is the strength of my life. Of whom shall I be afraid?" (Psalm 27:1). What gave Dr. King the courage and fortitude to face death? What gave David the courage he needed when he was pursued by King Saul and later by his own son Absalom?

We live in perilous times, in a dangerous world infected by the cancer of sin that leads all too many to commit senseless acts of violence. We may never face the malevolence of an assailant or even an assassin. Still, danger lurks. We never know when it may spring upon us or in what form. Knowing this causes fear. How then can we find the confidence to face it as courageously as David and Dr. King?

God was David's *light* and *salvation*. For David, God was a source of joy and peace, a steadying source of confidence. God gave him inspiration, understanding, and disciplined focus. God was also a safe refuge for him.

God is real and is vitally concerned about your welfare and safety as His child. Scripture tells us He knows the number of hairs on your head. Yes, we have fears, but we can bring them to our Almighty Father, who will walk us through every one of them. The one who formed you holds you in the very palms of His hands. He will never let you go no matter what comes against you.

You can go forward with confidence just as David and Dr. King did!

"I leave peace with you; I give to you My peace.
I do not give to you as the world gives. Do not
let your heart be troubled or let it be afraid."

JOHN 14:27

80. SAFE HOME

*But those who wait on the L*ORD ***shall*** *renew their strength.*
They shall mount up with wings like eagles, they shall run
and not be weary, and they shall walk and not faint.

ISAIAH 40:31

Will God come through with His promises? Proverbs 1:33 says, "But whoever listens to me *shall* dwell safely and *shall* be at peace without fear of evil" (emphasis added). Are we missing out on that peace?

Reread Proverbs 1:33, and watch for the condition to the promise. We need to *listen* to God and His wisdom for the promise to come into effect. If we ignore or avoid Him, we may not find ourselves at peace, and fears of evil may tear at our hearts.

So how do we listen to God? We need not search the universe for secret messages. God doesn't try to hide His will from us. He put it in His book, the Bible, which everyone has access to. He doesn't want peace to be impossible to find, but He insists that we find our peace not through political efforts or through well-meaning organizations. Whoever listens to him *shall* dwell safely and *shall* be at peace. Jesus is called the "Prince of Peace" (Isaiah 9:6). And peace is at hand if only we will seek it in Him.

When we read our Bibles attentively and regularly, we can find the safety and peace we are searching for. Having a quiet time with God isn't just a matter of Bible study for our heads; it's also peace for our hearts. As we learn more about God, we can place our troubles in His hands, knowing He will help us. God is at work in our lives in ways we may not even realize until later. He brings peace and turns back evil before it enters our lives.

Before we know it, God has brought us into a safe home that's filled with peace, and we are wonderfully blessed.

"I have spoken these things to you, that in Me you might have peace. In the world you shall have tribulation, but be of good cheer: I have overcome the world."
JOHN 16:33

81. LIFTED UP

But those who wait on the LORD shall renew their strength.
They shall mount up with wings like eagles, they shall run
and not be weary, and they shall walk and not faint.

ISAIAH 40:31

When we acknowledge the Lord, we're admitting that we ourselves are *not* the boss. Humility isn't something most of us enjoy. We like to think of ourselves as having at least some power in this world. Our society tells us we need to be confident in our own abilities, and that seems like a happier idea. But we quickly find it has its limitations when our confidence slips, and we are no longer as powerful as we'd like to be. Besides, no one can be confident in all things.

James 4:10 says, "Humble yourselves in the sight of the Lord, and He shall lift you up." God isn't telling us to humble ourselves to some other human being; we are to submit ourselves to *Him*. Though in other passages He commands us to submit to another person, such as a boss or a spouse, even then we are only doing so in obedience to God.

Humility before God shows that He is our Lord. We are not greater than He is. We understand that He rules our world, and nothing that happens to us here is beyond His control or repair. We look to Him for everything because we know He is ultimately in charge of our lives and deserves our obedience.

God's greatness shows us that even when we lack confidence in our own strength, we are not weak. The Lord comes alongside us and gives us strength as we wait on Him, trusting that all will work out.

Feeling a lack of confidence? Humble yourself before God. Seek His face and submit to His will, and though it may take some time, you will find yourself lifted up. Then you will be in the right place with the right confidence in your God who has put you there. When God sees us humbling ourselves to Him, He will not let us fail.

Humble yourselves therefore under the mighty hand of God, that He may exalt you in due time.
1 PETER 5:6

82. PERSPECTIVE

But those who wait on the LORD shall renew their strength.
They shall mount up with wings like eagles, they shall run
and not be weary, and they shall walk and not faint.

ISAIAH 40:31

Not all who lived a life of wholehearted dedication to our almighty Father and soared on eagles' wings were spared unfortunate and untimely deaths. Were *they* unprotected?

Why even bring this up? Aren't we who mount up on eagles' wings protected by God? Do we not live under the shadow of His wings of refuge? Yes, indeed! Then why would God make exceptions and make some like the mythical Icarus, who flew too close to the sun and fell to his death?

Jim Elliot, a zealous missionary to Ecuador, daringly sought out native tribes there for the sake of the gospel. Yet he and his companions were brutally murdered by those same natives. Why? John the Baptist was Messiah's herald, yet he ended up in prison—and was then beheaded. Why? Why would God allow these men who soared to suffer so? Did God abandon them? God has said that His ways are not our ways (Isaiah 55:8). His purposes often run contrary to how we would like things to be, but He never does anything without a purpose. And though it seems strange, His purpose always contributes to His glorious eternal plan of salvation. That's where faith comes in.

If we lived in a perfect world, we could expect God's perfect protection all the time. But we don't live in a perfect world. Far from it. We're able to mount up on eagles' wings, to run and not grow weary, to walk and not faint for a purpose. God's purpose. When we no longer are soaring on eagles' wings—maybe we're sidelined by an accident, a disease, a financial reversal, or a marital breakup—we can still *soar* on God's wings. Never forget: underneath us will be His everlasting arms carrying us upward (Deuteronomy 33:27).

They were stoned, they were sawed in two, were tempted, were slain with the sword. They wandered about in sheepskins and goatskins, being destitute, afflicted, tormented—of whom the world was not worthy.
HEBREWS 11:37–38

83. UNDER HIS WINGS

But those who wait on the LORD shall renew their strength.
*They shall mount up with **wings** like eagles, they shall run*
and not be weary, and they shall walk and not faint.

ISAIAH 40:31

Though Jerusalem was Israel's capital city, home to the temple where God was worshipped, it had a love-hate relationship with the Lord. Its inhabitants were proud of the temple, and its religious leaders could be very self-important about their positions. But when it came to obeying God and the prophets, the people of the city often fell far from God's will. When Jesus came to Jerusalem with His message of God's forgiveness and desire to be near to them, they rejected Him and even conspired to put Him to death.

As Jesus saw the city and its attitudes, it broke His heart: "O Jerusalem, Jerusalem, you who kill the prophets and stone those who are sent to you. How often I would have gathered your children together, even as a hen gathers her chickens under her wings, and you would not!" (Matthew 23:37).

Jesus wanted to gather these people under His wings and bring comfort and protection to them. He wanted to delight in their willingness to follow Him and worship the Father together. But just as they often refused the Father, they persecuted the Son. When He came to bring them salvation, they doubted that He was who He claimed to be, and most refused His message.

Just as He wanted to draw Jerusalem close and love the city, God wants to draw near to you too. He stretches out His wings to gather His beloved children to Him. But we have the option to find protection under His wings or stay outside where evil predators may carry us off to destruction. God offers safety, but He will not force us to accept it.

Our Lord wants a consistent love relationship with us. Just as a mother hen offers to protect her children every day, even multiple times a day, God offers Himself to us consistently.

Will we accept His offer?

But You, O Lord, are a shield for me,
my glory, and the lifter up of my head.
PSALM 3:3

84. WALKING IN GOD'S WAYS

But those who wait on the LORD shall renew their strength.
They shall mount up with wings like eagles, they shall run
*and not be weary, and they shall **walk** and not faint.*

ISAIAH 40:31

What does it mean to walk in the ways of God? In Deuteronomy 8:6, Moses told the Israelites, "You shall keep the commandments of the LORD your God, to walk in His ways and to fear Him." *Walk* here means to stay on a path in one continuous direction without deviating or wandering.

What are the ways of God? Two important ones are His way of righteousness and His way of holiness.

Righteousness can be defined as doing only that which is correct according to God's law. It generates good and beneficial results, those that are life enriching rather than damaging. Our motivation for walking in God's righteousness is to please Him in our thoughts, speech, and actions. Holiness can be defined as being set apart. Set apart from what? That's not the question. It's a matter of being set apart *for* something.

As disciples of Jesus, we are called to live in a manner that testifies both to the reality of God the Father's existence and

His saving work accomplished through Jesus. Jesus Himself said, "Therefore you be perfect [holy], even as your Father who is in heaven is perfect" (Matthew 5:48). Jesus will return, as He promised in scripture, to establish His eternal kingdom. Meanwhile, it is our task to make His Kingdom visible in the here and now.

We do that by conforming our lives to the example Jesus set for us. We want to walk as He walked. The Holy Spirit living within us empowers and enables us to anticipate Messiah's coming kingdom, honoring God the Father in our conduct despite our sin nature. However imperfectly, our character must reflect His.

This is how we walk in God's ways. Waiting on God allows us to walk without fainting.

For you were sometimes darkness, but now you are light in the Lord. Walk as children of light.
EPHESIANS 5:8

85. THE DESIRED HAVEN

*But those who wait on the L*ORD *shall renew their strength.*
*They shall **mount up** with wings like eagles, they shall run*
and not be weary, and they shall walk and not faint.

ISAIAH 40:31

A picturesque passage in the Psalms also uses the Hebrew verb translated "mount up" in Isaiah 40:31. It describes professional sailors who "mount up" on the wild waves of the sea—to the point that they fear for their lives:

> *Those who go down to the sea in ships, who do business*
> *in great waters, they see the works of the L*ORD *and*
> *His wonders in the deep. For He commands and*
> *raises the stormy wind, which lifts up its waves. They*
> *mount up to the heaven; they go down again to the*
> *depths. Their soul is melted because of trouble. They*
> *reel to and fro, and stagger like a drunken man, and*
> *are at their wits' end.*
>
> *Then they cry to the L*ORD *in their trouble, and*
> *He brings them out of their distresses. He makes the*
> *storm calm, so that its waves are still. Then they are*

glad because they are quiet, so He brings them to their
desired haven.

PSALM 107:23–30

It would seem that these sailors of the Psalms, "mounting up" in their creaking, groaning wooden ships, are quite a different crowd from "those who wait on the LORD" to renew their strength in Isaiah. And yet perhaps not.

Notice what happens when the sailors rise up to the heights of the waves only to crash back down to the depths, when their souls melt with fear and their reel to and fro: "they cry to the LORD in their trouble." And notice then how the Lord responds: "He brings them out of their distresses. He makes the storm calm, so that it's waves are still. . . . He brings them to their desired haven."

Whatever the cause of our trouble—whether it's simply the grinding weariness of life or it blows in like a raging storm—the solution is God. Wait on the Lord. Cry to the Lord. Keep the Lord first and foremost in your mind, and don't let go of Him. That's when you find your strength renewed and reach your desired haven.

Oh that men would praise the LORD for His goodness
and for His wonderful works to the children of men!
PSALM 107:31

86. WHERE STRENGTH ARISES

*But those who wait on the LORD shall renew their **strength**.*
They shall mount up with wings like eagles, they shall run
and not be weary, and they shall walk and not faint.

ISAIAH 40:31

Clearly, we have little strength compared to the Lord. We are not all-powerful. But that doesn't mean we should ignore the strength God has given us. Let's use the gift of our strength to the best of our ability and for the right purposes. God never gave us the power to create worlds, but in Him we can take part in changing ours.

When we come to Him, God enables us to love Him with our heart, soul, mind, and strength, which is to say with our entire being. Following Jesus cannot be half-hearted (Revelation 3:15–16). Either we commit to Him or we don't. And if we're not all in, know that there are no effective half measures to draw us close to God. It's impossible to keep one foot in our old way of life and another on His path.

It is a challenge to live wholeheartedly for God. Sin calls

our names, and we feel tempted to head in its direction. Though salvation is a one-time decision, living for God with all our strength goes on and on—it's a daily choice.

God knows our capabilities. He doesn't expect more of us than we can possibly give—though He may help us do much more than we think we can, and He will often challenge us in ways that exceed our strength. That just drives us to Him.

Jesus took the Ten Commandments and refined them into two. The first commandment, He told us, is to love our Lord by giving Him everything we have (Mark 12:30). And the second is to love our neighbors as ourselves (Mark 12:31). Putting our strength—the strength He gave us anyway—into both pleases our Lord and helps us walk in His way.

Know where your strength originates. It arises from God and serves to honor God.

"My grace is sufficient for you, for My strength is made perfect in weakness." Therefore, I will boast most gladly even more in my weaknesses, that the power of Christ may rest on me.

2 CORINTHIANS 12:9

87. A CENTURION'S EXAMPLE

*But those who wait on the **LORD** shall renew their strength.*
They shall mount up with wings like eagles, they shall run
and not be weary, and they shall walk and not faint.

ISAIAH 40:31

Roman centurions had a military obedience mindset. They were used to obeying the officers they reported to, and the men in their command had better hop to it when they gave orders. "I am a man under authority, having soldiers under me," one centurion said to Jesus. "And I say to this man, 'Go,' and he goes; and to another, 'Come,' and he comes; and to my servant, 'Do this,' and he does it" (Matthew 8:9).

This centurion understood that obedience wasn't a bad thing. In battle, it could mean the difference between life and death. But he was also humble enough to comprehend that in asking Jesus, a Jew, to heal his Gentile servant, he was stepping outside the usual boundaries. The centurion came from a pagan land, and his army had conquered Israel. His request for help could have easily been seen as an insult because the Jews did not take kindly to this double offense of religion and conquest.

But the servant was seriously ill, so the centurion braved going to Jesus. Obviously, he knew enough about Israel and Jewish religious practices that he recognized where the lines were drawn. Perhaps he'd even come to faith in the God of the Jews himself, considering Jesus' response to the soldier.

When Jesus offered to go see the servant, the centurion's military training clicked in, and he said that if Jesus simply said the word, the healing would take place. Amazed by such faith, the Lord healed the servant from a distance. . .and commended the Roman centurion's belief.

When we "wait on the Lord," we get renewed strength. Jesus is Lord of all (Acts 10:36). A Roman centurion, a stranger to God's people, understood this truth and acted upon it. Shouldn't we who are part of God's family through faith in Jesus do even more?

"Blessed are those who hear the word of God and keep it."
LUKE 11:28

88. THOUGHT MESSAGES

*But those who wait on the LORD shall **renew** their strength.*
They shall mount up with wings like eagles, they shall run
and not be weary, and they shall walk and not faint.

ISAIAH 40:31

Our world offers a lot of messages about how we should live, and many don't agree at all with scripture—they focus only on looking out for ourselves or pleasing people who aren't committed to God. Many worldly messages directly contradict the Bible. But because they constantly assault our ears, we can find ourselves believing them.

There is a worldly way of thinking and a godly way. The way our brain is most often filled with is the way we are likely to make part of our lives. That's why scripture warns us, "Do not be conformed to this world, but be transformed by the renewing of your mind, that you may prove what is that good and acceptable and perfect will of God" (Romans 12:2). Conforming to ungodly thinking will pressure us to go along with the crowd.

By contrast, biblical thinking—engaging in godly thoughts— renews our minds. When we come to Jesus, we experience a spiritual revolution that affects our whole being, including our minds.

But how we think and act depends on what we're feeding our minds; we need to put good things in our heads. If we're stuck in our old, pre-Jesus thought patterns, we can't make the most of the renewal He's brought into our lives. Trying to stay in the world with our heads and have Jesus in our hearts creates a divide that leads to trouble. We are neither comfortable in the world nor in Christ.

We will never live in God's perfect will if our hearts and heads aren't united in Christ. But in His perfect plan, God has provided the answer: we must allow the Spirit to transform our lives by renewing our minds. Changing our old way of thinking for godly thoughts proves His good, acceptable, and perfect will is occurring in our lives.

If you need help on this issue, perhaps memorize the following verse:

Finally, brothers, whatever things are true, whatever things are honest, whatever things are just, whatever things are pure, whatever things are lovely, whatever things are of good report, if there is any virtue, and if there is any praise, think on these things.
PHILIPPIANS 4:8

89. YOUR WINGS AWAIT

But those who wait on the LORD shall renew their strength.
*They shall mount up with **wings** like eagles, they shall run*
and not be weary, and they shall walk and not faint.

ISAIAH 40:31

Years ago, someone coined a saying that found its way onto T-shirts, coffee mugs, and note pads: "It's hard to soar like an eagle when you're surrounded by turkeys." Perhaps we as Christians shouldn't consider our fellow man a turkey. . .but we certainly understand the feeling of that wry message. In a world of selfish, dishonest, incompetent, and broken people, we'd love to just take wing and fly away, far up and above the mess at ground level.

That is the idea of Isaiah 40:31—in a world that drains our strength, there is an opportunity to rise above. The shepherd-boy-turned-king David longed for that opportunity as well. As he wrote in Psalm 55:1–6,

> *Give ear to my prayer, O God, and do not hide*
> *Yourself from my supplication.*
> *Attend to me, and hear me. I mourn in my*
> *complaint and make a noise,*

because of the voice of the enemy, because of the oppression of the wicked, for they cast iniquity on me, and in wrath they hate me.

My heart is greatly pained within me, and the terrors of death have fallen on me.

Fearfulness and trembling have come on me, and horror has overwhelmed me.

And I said, "Oh that I had wings like a dove! For then would I fly away and be at rest."

Eagles and doves are both God's creation, and He alone can grant us their wings. And just as Isaiah called on his readers to "wait on the Lord," David promised to "call on God. . .evening and morning and at noon I will pray and cry aloud, and He shall hear my voice" (Psalm 55:16–17). If calling out to God morning, noon, and evening isn't "waiting" on Him, what is?

Do what God commands and there will be a reward. Your wings await.

He has delivered my soul in peace from the battle that was against me, for there were many with me.
PSALM 55:18

90. THE LORD IS JUDGE

*But those who wait on the **LORD** shall renew their strength.*
They shall mount up with wings like eagles, they shall run
and not be weary, and they shall walk and not faint.

ISAIAH 40:31

We may call on God's name and declare He is our Lord, but the way we treat other believers reveals our true hearts.

Romans 14:10–12 says, "But why do you judge your brother? Or why do you despise your brother? For we shall all stand before the judgment seat of Christ. For it is written: 'As I live,' says the Lord, 'every knee shall bow to Me and every tongue shall confess to God.' So then every one of us shall give account of himself to God."

It's not hard to claim knowledge of God, but if we don't show it by our lives, our words don't mean much. When it comes to living with our Christian siblings, showing our faith becomes difficult when we have differing opinions on what we should—or shouldn't—do for God. It's easier to critique our brothers and sisters than to love them. But God doesn't call us to a critical spirit, and He hasn't appointed us to head up the judgment department.

It's not up to us to judge or despise our brother. We do not get to weigh in on his standing with God. That's up to Jesus. And if our brother has done something wrong, the Lord will set it right in eternity if not before. Until then, we need to trust in Him and treat our siblings lovingly. To do otherwise could destroy much of the good God has in mind for His church.

One day, all people, even those who have never accepted Christ, will recognize that He is Lord. They will bow down and confess that He is God and give account for their own faith or faithlessness (Philippians 2:9–11). When that day comes, each of us will be busy enough confessing our own failings without worrying about the failures of others.

Until then, trust that the Lord—the Judge—will decide correctly.

"Do not judge, that you not be judged. For with what judgment you judge, you shall be judged. And with what measure you use, it shall be measured to you again."
MATTHEW 7:1–2

91. THE MARATHON OF LIFE

But those who wait on the LORD shall renew their strength.
*They shall mount up with wings like eagles, they shall **run***
and not be weary, and they shall walk and not faint.

ISAIAH 40:31

It's been said that life is not a sprint—it's a marathon. The apostle Paul likened the Christian experience to a race (1 Corinthians 9:24), but it's clearly more than a 100-meter dash. Really, the life of faith is much more even than a 26-mile, 385-yard marathon. . .it's a nonstop endurance test that begins when we accept Christ and ends only when God calls us home to heaven.

The race of life was well described by the unknown author of the book of Hebrews. In a familiar passage, he wrote,

> *Since we also are surrounded by such a great cloud of witnesses, let us lay aside every weight, and the sin that so easily besets us, and let us run with patience the race that is set before us, looking to Jesus, the author and finisher of our faith, who for the joy that was set before Him endured the cross, despising the shame, and is seated at the right hand of the throne of*

God. For consider Him who endured such opposition
from sinners against Himself, lest you be wearied and
discouraged in your minds.

HEBREWS 12:1–3

Notice the consistency between the Old and New Testaments. Isaiah talks of our need to renew strength, of weariness and faintness in following God. The writer of Hebrews does the same for followers of Jesus, describing weights, besetting sins, enduring opposition, and weariness and discouragement.

But notice too the consistency of the prescription: "wait on the LORD" in Isaiah, "looking to Jesus" in Hebrews. As the author and finisher of our faith, He set the example of patient, persistent, ongoing obedience. Different descriptions, same idea, same benefit: by doing what God says, we gain His strength for the exhausting, frustrating, depressing challenges of life.

Therefore lift up the hands that hang down, and the
feeble knees, and make straight paths for your feet.
HEBREWS 12:12–13

92. REMAINING FAITHFUL

*But those who **wait** on the LORD shall renew their strength.*
They shall mount up with wings like eagles, they shall run
and not be weary, and they shall walk and not faint.

ISAIAH 40:31

Talk about waiting. . .

How long had Simeon been waiting to see "the consolation of Israel," Jesus Christ? Luke 2:25–26 doesn't say specifically, but you get the idea it had been a while: "And behold, in Jerusalem there was a man whose name was Simeon, and the same man was just and devout, waiting for the consolation of Israel, and the Holy Spirit was on him. And it was revealed to him by the Holy Spirit that he should not see death before he had seen the Lord's Christ."

For such a momentous occasion, he'd waited, probably with rising expectations. After all, Simeon knew one thing for sure—it would happen in his lifetime!

When God doesn't give us something quickly, we shouldn't think we'll never get it. In Simeon's case, the promised Messiah was just about to be born. God had planned it this way at a certain time, and nothing this man from Jerusalem could do would change that. But the promise was certainly going to be fulfilled.

What did Simeon do while he waited? He continued in all the daily things God called on him to do: following the law, sacrificing for his sins, giving to widows and orphans, and worshipping at the temple. Having to wait didn't mean he disregarded the commands of God in other areas. Simeon didn't become angry at God and stage a strike. He didn't try to tell God what His timing should be. Instead, he accepted God's promise and submitted to His will. Simeon was faithful.

Sometimes God makes us wait for a good thing. We may or may not know it's coming for certain, but we know we can trust Him. Whatever would be good for us is on its way. He will keep whatever isn't to our benefit at bay. But while we are waiting, are we remaining faithful?

Let us hold fast the profession of our faith without wavering, for He who promised is faithful.
HEBREWS 10:23

93. THERE'S ALWAYS MORE

*But those who wait on the L*ORD *shall renew their strength.*
They shall mount up with wings like eagles, they shall run
*and not be weary, and they shall walk **and** not faint.*

Isaiah 40:31

When you serve an infinite God, you enjoy infinite blessing. It would be a wonderful gift of grace to be able simply to walk through this difficult world without fainting. But God gives more: we can run without experiencing weariness. And beyond that, we get to "mount up with wings like eagles," rising above every disappointment, distress, and disaster.

When we follow God humbly and obediently, there's always an *and*. He adds more and more to our semi-trailer of blessings to the point that it overflows. Not so sure about that? Check out these promises:

- "You prepare a table before me in the presence of my enemies. You anoint my head with oil. My cup runs over" (Psalm 23:5).

- "Blessed be the Lord, who daily loads us with benefits, even the God of our salvation" (Psalm 68:19).

- "'Behold, the days are coming,'" says the LORD, "when the plowman shall overtake the reaper, and the treader of grapes him who sows seed'" (Amos 9:13).

- "'Bring all your tithes into the storehouse, that there may be food in My house, and test Me now in this,'" says the LORD of hosts, "'if I will not open the windows of heaven for you and pour out a blessing for you, that there will not be enough room to receive it'" (Malachi 3:10).

- "Give, and it shall be given to you. Good measure—pressed down, and shaken together, and running over—shall be given by men into your bosom. For with the same measure that you use, it shall be measured back to you" (Luke 6:38).

- "Now to Him who is able to do exceedingly abundantly above all that we ask or think, according to the power that works in us, to Him be glory in the church by Christ Jesus throughout all ages, world without end. Amen" (Ephesians 3:20–21).

God's *and*s are your blessings. Serve Him faithfully. You'll find there's always more.

"I have come that they might have life, and that they might have it more abundantly."

JOHN 10:10

94. WHAT KIND OF LORD?

But those who wait on the LORD shall renew their strength.
They shall mount up with wings like eagles, they shall run
and not be weary, and they shall walk and not faint.

ISAIAH 40:31

The idea of having a lord may not appeal to the independent Western mind-set. In nations that allow people to vote on their governmental officials, the idea isn't very relatable.

But the Lord Jesus isn't any ordinary king or prime minister or president. He doesn't force our children into His armies to defend His nation. He's no heavy-handed, greedy ruler who simply wants His own way. We never have to fear that His laws will be unfair or that He will mistreat us. All His laws are just (Deuteronomy 32:4).

Instead, Jesus is the Lord through whom we received atonement, as Romans 5:11 says. We were made right with God through His sacrifice. What earthly lord has done such a thing—or even could do it if he wanted to?

And one day our Lord will come again to rule eternally and perfectly (Hebrews 9:28; 1 Thessalonians 4:16–17).

We trust in Jesus for our salvation, so we can trust Him for everything else, can't we?

What kind of Lord do we want? A yes-man who tells us what we want to hear? Or someone who really can save us, here on earth *and* for eternity? "This is the will of Him who sent Me, that everyone who sees the Son and believes in Him may have everlasting life. And I will raise him up on the last day" (John 6:40). Scripture shows us our powerful Lord, one whom we are meant to follow, not dictate to.

Jesus' rule shouldn't make us unhappy—if it does, we need to reconsider our commitment to Him. He has certainly made a powerful commitment to us! Serving Jesus should be a delight, even if we have to go through uncomfortable times here on earth.

What kind of Lord do you have?

Serve the LORD with gladness; come before His presence with singing. Know that the LORD, He is God. It is He who has made us, and not we ourselves; we are His people, and the sheep of His pasture.

PSALM 100:2–3

95. HEALING WINGS

But those who wait on the LORD shall renew their strength.
*They shall mount up with **wings** like eagles, they shall run*
and not be weary, and they shall walk and not faint.

ISAIAH 40:31

God has a thing for wings. He'll provide them for you. And He'll use His own to protect you.

When the Messiah, "the Sun of righteousness" (Malachi 4:2) appears, His wings will bring healing to His people. This expression can also mean "sun of vindication," which seems appropriate since the first verse of Malachi 4 describes the destruction of the wicked.

As in many places in scripture, this passage compares the wages of wickedness with those of love for God. The wicked will burn up on the coming and terrifying day of the Lord, while those who fear God will experience the healing of the Sun of righteousness. The later part of verse 2 reads, "You will go out and frolic like well-fed calves" (NIV). Like young cows released into a field on a sunny day, we will rejoice and flourish, while the wicked become nothing more than ashes under our feet.

Does it bother you that the wicked seem to flourish despite

their lack of love for God? You aren't the only one. That was often a lament in the psalms too (Psalm 37:1–2, Psalm 92:7, Psalm 94:3). But don't sweat it. Psalm 1:4–5 promises that they "are like the chaff that the wind drives away. Therefore the ungodly shall not stand in the judgment nor sinners in the congregation of the righteous." Whether they are compared to chaff or ashes, God tells us twice that the wicked will not last. And Psalm 1:6 continues the thought: "For the Lord knows the way of the righteous, but the way of the ungodly shall perish."

Healing wings are protecting the righteous. Wait on the Lord, and you're completely safe.

And who is he that will harm you if
you are followers of what is good?
1 Peter 3:13

96. WAIT IN HOPE

*But those who **wait** on the LORD shall renew their strength.*
They shall mount up with wings like eagles, they shall run
and not be weary, and they shall walk and not faint.
ISAIAH 40:31

God has given us His salvation, and we rejoice in that. But like a woman birthing a child, we experience pain along with our rejoicing. Knowing Jesus is delightful doesn't mean every situation in this life will be.

That wasn't the apostle Paul's experience, and it won't be ours either. But at the same time that Paul suffered indignities from those who objected to the gospel, he was also greatly blessed with a mission that brought many Gentiles into the kingdom. And in heaven, he will receive a great reward.

As we await the coming of our King, we and all of God's creation feel the influence of sin in our world. Though Jesus died for our sin, He has not yet completely removed it from Earth. In Genesis 3:17–18, God let Adam know that he and Eve weren't the only ones who would suffer for their sin. The entire planet had been changed by their wrongdoing. Since then, all humanity has felt the impact of the curse.

When we accept Jesus, we know the joy of redemption as our hearts are changed. But it doesn't take long for us to recognize that while *we* have become new, the rest of the world hasn't. We have accepted our Savior, with all the blessing that entails—but the rest of the world lives with blinders on. And we ourselves still struggle with the sin that clings to us. As we fight against our old nature, we wait for the final adoption, the redemption of our body.

Redemption is coming. Just don't lose hope.

For we know that the whole creation groans and labors in pain together until now. And not only that, but also we ourselves who have the firstfruits of the Spirit, even we ourselves groan within ourselves, waiting for the adoption—namely, the redemption of our body.

ROMANS 8:22–23

97. STRENGTH TO RUN AND LEAP

But those who wait on the LORD shall renew their strength.
*They shall mount up with wings like eagles, they shall **run***
and not be weary, and they shall walk and not faint.

ISAIAH 40:31

Following God's deliverance of Israel from the Philistines, when God "had delivered him out of the hand of all his enemies" (2 Samuel 22:1), David sang a chapter-long worship song describing the ways God had protected him and saved him from violence. Clearly, from his song's descriptions, the anointed but uncrowned king experienced many instances of fearfulness and doubt.

Becoming king wasn't just a matter of planning a coronation. David had to fight for his throne against the spiritually failed King Saul. Then he had to battle neighboring countries to confirm his throne. When God brought David into the place He'd promised him, David rose up on eagles' wings with praise.

But David didn't just worship God when times looked especially good. Throughout his efforts to gain the throne,

David praised God. Understanding the power of praise, David worshipped God consistently throughout his life and wrote more than seventy psalms.

Sometimes, in prayer, he tussled with the Lord over the wicked (Psalm 11) or his own trials (Psalm 13). But the end of these psalms converts a difficult situation into one of trust in and worship of God. David remained steadfast, always turning his thoughts and hope toward God.

He admitted that His reward included effort on his part: "The LORD rewarded me according to my righteousness. He has repaid me according to the cleanness of my hands. For I have kept the ways of the LORD and have not wickedly departed from my God" (2 Samuel 22:21–22).

Like David, have you made praise and worship a regular part of your life? Do you trust God through every difficulty? If so, He will renew your strength to accomplish great things.

For by You I have run through a troop.
By my God I have leaped over a wall.
2 SAMUEL 22:30

98. SPIRITUAL MUSCLES

*But those who wait on the LORD shall renew their **strength**. They shall mount up with wings like eagles, they shall run and not be weary, and they shall walk and not faint.*

ISAIAH 40:31

Our strength doesn't lie in ourselves, but in God. That should be fairly obvious. We struggle to find enough energy to get through our workdays when there are many demands on our time. We need spiritual power to hold our tongues when someone speaks irritating words. We need patience with our family. The challenges to our strength are many, and we're easily worn out. We need a strength renewal on a daily basis.

Where do we turn? People may help a bit. Talking out a situation can help. But scripture encourages us to seek the Lord. We can glory in His strength when we have a close connection with God. As 1 Chronicles 16:10–12 says, "Glory in His holy name; let the hearts of those who seek the LORD rejoice. Seek the LORD and His strength; seek His face continually. Remember His marvelous works that He has done, His wonders and the judgments of His mouth."

In this passage, *glory* means "praise"—and as we appreciate and honor God's powerful nature, we connect with His strength. Our hearts rejoice in the truth of who He is and what He has done for us.

Over and over, scripture encourages us to remember what God has done for us. How has His power been working in our lives? Has He turned us from a besetting sin? Then we know He can give us strength to reply peaceably to someone who's trying to upset us. Has He helped our marriage when it was in difficulty? He can bring us through another rough spot. The God who has given us strength in the past offers it again now as we seek His direction and avoid sin.

Working our spiritual muscles adds His strength to ours. Trials are like the weights we lift or the course we run. They can bring us strength as we stand firm in God's truth and declare His glory.

But we all, with open faces, looking as in a mirror at the glory of the Lord, are being changed into the same image from glory to glory, even as by the Spirit of the Lord.
2 Corinthians 3:18

99. ALL THE STRENGTH

*But those who wait on the LORD shall renew their **strength**. They shall mount up with wings like eagles, they shall run and not be weary, and they shall walk and not faint.*

ISAIAH 40:31

Do you feel surrounded by powerful, evil enemies who seek to destroy you? Take heart. Their power is nothing compared to God's. He who created the foundations of the world cannot be ignored or avoided. No wicked thing can do an end run around Him.

Sometimes our enemies seem nameless. Life is simply troubling. *Is it the wiles of God's enemy, Satan, or my own failings?* we each may ask ourselves. At other times, the enemy is a clearly defined, human entity. Maybe he's trying to cause harm or maybe it's unintentional—either way, we're up against trouble.

God's power exceeds everything, though. Nothing in the world can overwhelm Him. Satan, with all his power to tempt, did not make the world and cannot overthrow it. Jesus destroyed Satan through His own death (Hebrews 2:14) and will one day throw him into a lake of fire, along with death and hell (Revelation 20:10, 14).

Humans cannot "prevail by strength" (1 Samuel 2:9), because their power is miniscule by comparison to the one who makes His people "mount up with wings like eagles."

When we feel less than powerful, let's remember that God provides strength. We need to call on Him for aid. He watches over the feet of His saints so they need not take a wrong step. And He silences the wicked.

Our Father God has given strength to King Jesus and exalted Him. Through Him we have all the muscle we need.

You have enlarged my steps under me, so my feet did not slip.
Psalm 18:36

100. THERE'S ONLY ONE

*But those who wait on **the** Lord shall renew their strength.*
They shall mount up with wings like eagles, they shall run
and not be weary, and they shall walk and not faint.

ISAIAH 40:31

If you conducted a survey of committed Christian men, hopefully every last one of them would say there is no other God but the Lord. As King David put it, "All the gods of the people are idols, but the Lord made the heavens" (1 Chronicles 16:26). Our God is not *a* god. . .He is *the* one true God.

Even committed Christian men are susceptible to temptation and sin, however. So even though we say we believe in "*the* Lord," oftentimes we're distracted by other things. Our careers maybe. Perhaps a relationship. Our health and fitness. A hot car or fancy house. It would seem to go without saying that none of these things will ultimately satisfy.

But we're going to say it anyway.

Only those men who "wait on the Lord" will find renewed strength. Only those men who wait on the Lord mount up with wings like eagles. Only those men who wait on the Lord can run without weariness and walk without fainting. Reminders aren't bad things. As the apostle Paul told the believers of Philippi, "To write the same things to you, to me indeed is not grievous, but for you it is safe" (Philippians 3:1).

So take a moment today to reaffirm your belief in *the* Lord. Our God is the creator and keeper of the universe. He is the all-knowing, all-powerful, all-present God who is sovereign over all things. Nothing compares to Him, and we should quickly shoot down any thought that tries to make an equivalence.

There's only one God, the God who made you, knows you, loves you, and offers you His strength.

"I am the LORD, and there is no one else. There is no God besides Me. I girded you, though you have not known Me, that they may know from the rising of the sun, and from the west, that there is no one besides Me. I am the LORD, and there is no one else."
ISAIAH 45:5–6

101. RUNNING TO JESUS

But those who wait on the LORD shall renew their strength.
*They shall mount up with wings like eagles, they shall **run***
and not be weary, and they shall walk and not faint.

ISAIAH 40:31

Isaiah 40:31 is written to people who already know and follow the Lord. But it begs a question: Shouldn't those of us who enjoy God's benefits try to share them with others? The unsaved are slogging through life too with a dark eternity in view.

In the book of Genesis, God called a people to Himself through Abraham. Ultimately, the nation of Israel was founded to worship the Lord. But the Israelites were inconsistent in their devotion. So God called people who were not from Israel: "Everyone who thirsts, come to the waters, and he who has no money, come, buy and eat" (Isaiah 55:1). Isaiah 55:5 tells us they ran to Him.

Look at the world today, and you can see the impact Christianity has had. The apostle Paul was called to reach the Gentiles, and God began to fulfill the prophecy of Isaiah 55.

By the end of the Bible, we read of a new song sung to the Lamb of God, Jesus, in heaven: "You are worthy to take the book and to open its seals, for You were slain and have redeemed us to God by Your blood out of every family, and tongue, and people, and nation" (Revelation 5:9). God left out no tribe or people group, and no language is a barrier to salvation. "And this gospel of the kingdom shall be preached in all the world as a witness to all nations," Jesus declared (Matthew 24:14). All people need salvation, and God has opened the doors to anyone who will come in. Not one person is left out of the invitation.

Though we may feel uncomfortable sharing the gospel because some people will say no, God tells us to share anyway. Yes, some will refuse, but others will run toward Jesus. It's not up to us to decide who will respond well and who won't. God wants His good news made available to everyone. Will we be the conduits of His incredible offer?

But as we were allowed by God to be entrusted
with the gospel, even so we speak—not as
pleasing men, but God, who tries our hearts.
1 THESSALONIANS 2:4

102. DRENCHED IN DEEP WATERS?

*But those who **wait** on the LORD shall renew their strength.*
They shall mount up with wings like eagles, they shall run
and not be weary, and they shall walk and not faint.

Isaiah 40:31

Waiting doesn't always come at convenient times. In fact, waiting for God is almost invariably in the toughest times of life. And in many of those cases, God seems to be silent.

The psalmist David knew something about the overwhelming feelings of stress and loneliness. "I sink in deep mire, where there is no standing," he lamented. "I have come into deep waters, where the floods overflow me. I am weary of my crying; my throat is dried; my eyes fail while I wait for my God" (Psalm 69:2–3).

In such times, like David, we may wonder if God has heard our prayers. Waiting tends to exacerbate our fears. If we had no fear at all, waiting would be simple. But what need do we have to fear when we have this promise? "Do not fear, for I am with you. Do not be dismayed, for I am your God. I will strengthen you. Yes, I will help you. Yes, I will uphold you with My righteous right hand" (Isaiah 41:10).

We need not fear what any human can do to us: "He has said, 'I will never leave you or forsake you.' So we may boldly say, 'The Lord is my helper, and I will not fear what man shall do to me'" (Hebrews 13:5–6). Our God is even in charge of the natural world's earthquakes, tornadoes, and floods that threaten us. In fact, nothing can go beyond God's knowledge, power, and care. "Cast your burden on the LORD, and He shall sustain you; He shall never allow the righteous to be moved" (Psalm 55:22).

When the floods of the world threaten us, waiting may seem hard. But the God who has promised is always faithful. Though we wait, we can count on His support. He may come through at the eleventh hour, but God never neglects us.

Humble yourselves therefore under the mighty hand of God, that He may exalt you in due time, casting all your care upon Him, for He cares for you.
1 PETER 5:6–7

103. IS HE LORD?

*But those who wait on the **LORD** shall renew their strength.*
They shall mount up with wings like eagles, they shall run
and not be weary, and they shall walk and not faint.

Isaiah 40:31

To some people, Jesus is a nice teacher. They like some of the positive things He said, but ask them to make Him the Lord of their lives, and they won't understand why you'd even say that. Nice teachers have good ideas, but they just offer guidelines to follow.

Others may admit that perhaps Jesus is a prophet who has special knowledge of God, but they'd find it a long stretch to believe in His divinity. Maybe they too like some of His ideas, but bending the knee to Him as God is another matter.

Certainly, if Jesus were simply a man, those kinds of ideas would be appropriate. Putting all your eggs in a mere human's basket is dangerous. Even the wisest men fail sometimes. But Jesus never failed and never fails. Philippians 2:6–8 makes it clear that He was fully God and fully man—a combination that meant He was perfect and made salvation possible. He's not just an ordinary, fallible human being.

When Jesus was raised from the dead, it proved His divinity. Our acceptance of such a truth takes an understanding of our sin. When we recognize our own imperfections and our need for a savior (Romans 3:21–26), we enter the territory in which we can accept His lordship. Once our hearts comprehend that we cannot measure up to God, we become humble enough to understand our great need for His grace through faith in Jesus. Then we can confess that He alone can save us.

When we know our need and declare Jesus as the Lord of our lives, God is faithful to save and strengthen us.

For there is one God and one mediator between God and men, the man Christ Jesus, who gave Himself as a ransom for all, to be testified in due time.
1 TIMOTHY 2:5–6

104. GOD'S STRENGTH ON DISPLAY

*But those who wait on the LORD shall renew their **strength**.
They shall mount up with wings like eagles, they shall run
and not be weary, and they shall walk and not faint.*

ISAIAH 40:31

Following the Exodus, God knew the children of the Hebrew people needed to remember the event. So He proclaimed that His people should have a day of commemoration of their freedom, which would be passed down from generation to generation. As time went by and memories became vague, younger people would say, "What is this?" to which the reply would be, "By strength of hand the LORD brought us out from Egypt, from the house of bondage" (Exodus 13:14).

"What is this?" is still asked in Jewish families by the youngest person at the Passover Seder each year. The question is an opportunity to revisit the story of the migration of Israel into their land of promise. And it's a chance for the senior members of the family to share the greatness and strength of God, who brought His people out of Egypt, the most powerful nation in the world at the time, even though Pharaoh resisted for so long. But no power on earth stops God's plans.

Israel couldn't claim that their strength made the Exodus happen, and Moses certainly didn't try to say that it happened because of his wisdom. Bringing thousands of people through the desert to a new land took more than anything the prophet could have arranged. So every year, Israel commemorates the greatness and salvation of God.

God's strength hasn't changed. And now we have an even clearer picture of salvation in the sacrifice and resurrection of Jesus. How much more reason do we Christians have to rejoice in God's strength?

That strength is readily available to anyone who waits on the Lord. Why wouldn't you want to access such strength in your life?

The Lord stood with me and strengthened me,
that by me the preaching might be fully known
and that all the Gentiles might hear.
2 TIMOTHY 4:17

105. THE ONLY WORTHY ACCOMPLISHMENT

But those who wait on the LORD shall renew their strength.
*They shall **mount up** with wings like eagles, they shall run*
and not be weary, and they shall walk and not faint.

ISAIAH 40:31

One challenge of the Christian faith is finding the dividing line between God's work and our own. Of course, He is completely sovereign and accomplishes whatever He pleases, however He pleases. But somehow, in ways known fully only to Him, God has given human beings a free will, the ability to choose when and how and to what extent we will obey, honor, and serve Him. If that seems mysterious, it is!

Isaiah 40:31 calls us to "wait on the LORD." That is a responsibility that falls on us. If we follow through, our strength is renewed, and we'll mount up with wings like eagles. The unstated implication of the verse is that the strengthening and the mounting up come to us *from God*. We can't really generate that kind of blessing on our own, and we should never assume we can. The prophet Jeremiah showed what happened to Babylon, when the proud nation thought it could rise up in its own strength.

"Behold, the days are coming," the Lord told His prophet, "that I will bring judgment on her idols, and the wounded shall groan through all her land. Though Babylon should mount up to heaven, and though she should fortify the height of her strength, yet destroyers shall come to her from Me" (Jeremiah 51:52–53).

No matter how smart, strong, good-looking, or successful we may be, we'll never find lasting success apart from God. Maybe we'll "mount up" for a time, but if our high flying doesn't start with God or honor Him, it will certainly end.

The only worthy accomplishment of this life is waiting on the Lord. Then He'll make sure we have renewed strength and eagles' wings.

For this is what the high and lofty One who inhabits eternity, whose name is Holy, says: "I dwell in the high and holy place, also with him who is of a contrite and humble spirit, to revive the spirit of the humble and to revive the heart of the contrite ones."

ISAIAH 57:15

106. WAIT WITH EXPECTATION

*But those who **wait** on the LORD shall renew their strength.*
They shall mount up with wings like eagles, they shall run
and not be weary, and they shall walk and not faint.

ISAIAH 40:31

When God doesn't send answers to our most pressing questions or issues, how long do we hold on?

It's not that we cannot ask for help from other people while we wait. Support from godly folks can be a real encouragement, and God approves of mutual aid among Christian siblings (James 2:14–17). Getting help from other Christians may even be part of our waiting, but if we rely too much on human aid, we may miss the bigger picture. No individual believer has all of God's wisdom at his fingertips—but where human help fails, God's is always available. Ultimately, our hope lies in what *God* can do for us, not what anyone else can devise to solve our problems.

When waiting seems to last so long that we feel we can't go any further, it's time to abide in the Lord just a bit longer (John 15:4–5). No matter how long God asks you to wait, stand firm in your love for Him. He has a purpose for the waiting, be sure of that. It's not that He cannot or will not act.

As we wait, God builds our expectation. We know that He blesses His people (Psalm 1:1; 3:8; 32:1; 34:8). He commands us to trust in Him while promising to direct our paths (Proverbs 3:5–6). So, as we wait for Him alone, we know we do not have unrealistic expectations. God *wants* us to place our trust in His hands. As we believe and look expectantly toward Him, our excitement rises as we wait to see just how He will come to our aid in tight circumstances.

Waiting does not need to be a time of pain. Let's think about the good things God has promised and put our trust in Him. It may not happen as soon as we wish (what ever does?), but the promise stands: "Those who wait on the LORD shall renew their strength. They shall mount up with wings like eagles, they shall run and not be weary, and they shall walk and not faint."

My soul, wait for God alone,
for my expectation is from Him.
PSALM 62:5

107. WALKING ON HIGH PLACES

But those who wait on the LORD shall renew their strength.
They shall mount up with wings like eagles, they shall run
*and not be weary, and they shall **walk** and not faint.*

ISAIAH 40:31

Habakkuk 3:19 describes the blessing God gives His people in a delightful way similar to Isaiah's picture of eagle wings: "The LORD God is my strength, and He will make my feet like deer's feet, and He will make me walk on my high places." As deer's feet that are able to climb mountains with ease in God's strength, we can take on the high, rocky places of our emotions without trouble. Similar to the surefooted deer, we dart over rocks and plant our feet on the roughest places with assurance.

In our own strength, we would stumble over rocks, slip and slide, and certainly not make it up the steepest hills. But in God's power, we can shoot over a nearly vertical rock face or carefully pick our way along a mountaintop.

But if we become proud of our own spiritual abilities, we may soon find ourselves sliding back to the bottom of the mountain.

The psalmist makes it clear that it is God who "sets me on my high places" (Psalm 18:33). It is *always* God who gives us the strength to make spiritual headway, bring people to Himself, and teach others to live in Him. Though we may work hard and consistently for His kingdom, His Spirit always lies behind our success. He is the one who fills us and enables us to take on tasks.

When a deer moves up a mountainside, he does so effortlessly. He isn't comparing himself to other animals or thinking how much better he'd be if he were more like another deer. Keeping his eyes on the goal, he heads up the mountain in confidence.

To walk on the high places, without stumbling or fainting, our confidence must be in the Lord's strength, never our own. May we never ruin the waiting we did before by feeling proud of ourselves.

In the fear of the LORD is strong confidence,
and His children shall have a place of refuge.
PROVERBS 14:26

108. GOD'S *NOTS*

But those who wait on the LORD shall renew their strength.
They shall mount up with wings like eagles, they shall run
*and **not** be weary, and they shall walk and not faint.*

ISAIAH 40:31

Some business leaders forbid the use of *but* in a discussion of ideas. They believe the term is too negative and squelches conversation. The phrase "yes, and" is preferred.

But. . .there are times when a negative is necessary. *Not* is one of those words, and in Isaiah 40:31, it provides a vital contrast. Those who wait on the Lord get to run and not be weary. They get to walk and not faint.

Throughout scripture, God provides other notable *nots*. Here are just a few:

- "If you do well, shall you not be accepted?" (Genesis 4:7).

- "And, behold, the word of the LORD came to [Abraham], saying, 'This [servant] shall not be your heir, but he who shall come forth out of your own body shall be your heir'" (Genesis 15:4).

- "And the angel of the LORD said to [Sarah], 'I will multiply your descendants exceedingly, that it shall not be numbered for multitude'" (Genesis 16:10).

- "Now therefore, do not be grieved or angry with yourselves that you sold me here, for God sent me before you to preserve life" (Genesis 45:5).

- "And when I see the blood, I will pass over you, and the plague shall not be on you to destroy you when I strike the land of Egypt" (Exodus 12:13).

- "Those who know Your name will put their trust in You, for You, LORD, have not forsaken those who seek You" (Psalm 9:10).

- "They cried to You and were delivered. They trusted in You and were not confounded" (Psalm 22:5).

In multiplication, two negatives result in a positive. In life, applying God's *not* to our negative turns everything around. If you're in a place of weariness right now, Isaiah 40:31 provides the change you crave.

Though an army should encamp
against me, my heart shall not fear.
PSALM 27:3

109. LORD OF FINANCE

*But those who wait on the **LORD** shall renew their strength.*
They shall mount up with wings like eagles, they shall run
and not be weary, and they shall walk and not faint.

ISAIAH 40:31

Do we rise up with eagles' wings when it comes to money? Or is that the only place we seem totally earthbound?

We may experience spiritual blessings, have a successful ministry, and enjoy our work. God may have called us to the Christian life, a good marriage, and a solid career, but paying bills each month may remain a trial. A Christian man may even argue with his wife about money. Sometimes a couple's relationship to money falls into the "love/hate" category.

Money and how we use it tells us a lot about our faith. Jesus knew that the rich young ruler was spiritually bankrupt and didn't much care about people. The Lord told him to sell his goods and give to the poor (Matthew 19). This kind of radical spiritual surgery isn't necessary for everyone. Jesus isn't recommending permanent poverty for all Christians, but it does show us that losing everything isn't the end of the world; it may be the beginning of hope for our spiritual lives.

In 1 Timothy 6:17, the apostle Paul gave Timothy a warning about his most wealthy congregants: "Charge those who are rich in this world not to be haughty or trust in uncertain riches but to trust in the living God, who richly gives us all things to enjoy."

Our attitude toward money takes our spiritual trust temperature. Instead of hoarding our wealth, Jesus tells us to give to those who ask (Matthew 5:42) and store up heavenly treasures (Matthew 6:19–21). When we do that, we show where our faith truly lies. Is Jesus really the Lord of our lives? Do we trust in God, and are we content with what He gives?

Let your conduct be without covetousness, and be content with what you have, for He has said, "I will never leave you or forsake you." So we may boldly say, "The Lord is my helper, and I will not fear what man shall do to me."

HEBREWS 13:5–6

110. NEW LORD

*But those who wait on the LORD shall **renew** their strength.*
They shall mount up with wings like eagles, they shall run
and not be weary, and they shall walk and not faint.

ISAIAH 40:31

Even if you don't quite believe you are worthy of the salvation God has given you, He thinks you are—and He encourages you to walk with Him in a new way. Though you could have never earned a relationship with Him, the Lord "has made us suitable to be partakers of the inheritance of the saints in light" (Colossians 1:12).

Once we know Jesus, a lifestyle change is in order, not to earn God's favor—we already have that—but to give thanks for all our new Lord has given us and to please Him. He delivered us from the power of darkness. Our translation into the kingdom of heaven means we walk on a renewed path, one of fruitful works that glorify Him instead of ourselves.

We grow in desire to know more of our new Lord—something that never would have crossed our minds before our salvation—and draw close to Him in Bible study and prayer. This new life of salvation is not without troubles; it requires patience and long-suffering. Yet He strengthens us for every trial and enables us to withstand them so we can inherit eternal life.

Even after we've walked with the Lord for a while, it's possible to become discouraged. Just remember that He is the one who qualified you. And He will deliver you from every power of darkness if you call out to Him today. In the Lord, you have been renewed—and by waiting on Him, you possess all the strength you need for the rest of your life.

He has chosen us in Him before the foundation of the world, that we should be holy and without blame before Him in love, having predestined us to the adoption of children by Jesus Christ to Himself.
EPHESIANS 1:4–5

111. WHERE ARE YOU RUNNING?

But those who wait on the LORD shall renew their strength.
*They shall mount up with wings like eagles, they shall **run***
and not be weary, and they shall walk and not faint.

ISAIAH 40:31

The New Testament Galatians began their spiritual life well. But people called Judaizers came to their congregation, insisting they had to be circumcised to follow God faithfully.

That was certainly not the apostle Paul's teaching. But the people began to trust the message of those Jews who tried to turn them from the grace Paul preached toward obedience to the Old Testament law. They flipped the Galatians from the truth to a practice that was unnecessary and deceptive, denying the liberty Jesus had bought through His sacrifice (Galatians 5:13).

"You ran well," Paul wrote to them. "Who hindered you that you should not obey the truth?" (Galatians 5:7). Like a long-distance runner who gets distracted by something along the route, the Galatians allowed faulty doctrine to lead them astray.

Does doctrine matter? Many people today would like to say

it doesn't. "I know Jesus," they say. "Isn't that all that matters?"

Paul was happy the Galatians knew the Lord, but he would not have denied the importance of doctrine. It doesn't just matter *that* you believe; *what* you believe is also vital. In this case, Paul wasn't concerned that the Galatians were lax in their faith; he worried that they had not held fast to their freedom in Christ.

Like the Galatians, we need to beware those who would add to the commands of scripture, making them either too strict or too freewheeling. Either doctrinal mistake can lead us into trouble.

Wait on the Lord by searching out His truth in scripture. Then you will understand where you are running and why you are on that course. It's the way to run well.

Your word is a lamp to my feet and a light to my path.
PSALM 119:105

112. IS SEEING BELIEVING?

*But those who **wait** on the LORD shall renew their strength.*
They shall mount up with wings like eagles, they shall run
and not be weary, and they shall walk and not faint.

ISAIAH 40:31

You've heard it said "Seeing is believing," but that's not necessarily true. Seeing is seeing, and it requires little or no faith—unless you have reason not to believe what's before your eyes, then even seeing is accompanied by doubt.

Faith is about believing what we don't see. We have faith in many ordinary earthly things. Yet if they failed us, we might not be surprised.

But trusting God for our eternal future is a much larger issue, one we wait for much longer and have a lot more invested in. We come to Christ, having heard the gospel, hoping and trusting it is true. And as time goes on and we walk with God, He confirms our faith in remarkable ways.

Hebrews 11:1: "Now faith is the substance of things hoped for, the evidence of things not seen." Get that? Faith is your evidence of the truth you've experienced about God. As you wait for the fulfillment of all His promises, you have hope and wait patiently. And the longer you wait, the more you are convinced of His truth and hope in it.

Waiting is simply the time between our first belief and the time when we see God and His truths fulfilled. It tests our faith to see if we can patiently hold on while God brings His plans to fulfillment. Waiting does *not* indicate that His promises will never come to pass.

God's promise in Isaiah 40:31 tells us our waiting will not be in vain. We will see our hopes fulfilled as we rise up in flight. This is where hope leads us, and we can be confident that waiting leads to our happy ending.

For we are saved in hope, but hope that is seen is not hope. For why does a man still hope for what he sees? But if we hope for what we do not see, then we wait for it with patience.
ROMANS 8:24–25

113. PLEASING RIGHTEOUSNESS

But those who wait on the LORD shall renew their strength.
They shall mount up with wings like eagles, they shall run
and not be weary, and they shall walk and not faint.

ISAIAH 40:31

When He created the world, the Lord God had a plan. Not just one that brought mountains and plains into existence and filled them with wildlife, but one that included human beings, who would inhabit the earth and live righteously for Him. Even "the heavens declare the glory of God, and the heavens proclaim His handiwork" to His people (Psalm 19:1).

Imagine creating the entire world and heavens to bring people into communion with yourself! God spared no effort; it was that important to Him to bring you into His kingdom. And He doesn't consider it wasted effort: "This is what the LORD says, who created the heavens—God Himself, who formed the earth and made it. He has established it. He did not create it in vain. He formed it to be inhabited: 'I am the LORD, and there is no one else'" (Isaiah 45:18).

Nor did the Lord create mankind with an intent to frustrate their search for Him. Jeremiah 29:13 promises: "And you shall seek Me and find Me, when you search for Me with all your heart." Though He may sometimes seem to hide Himself (Isaiah 45:15), He also reveals Himself to those who honestly search. The prophet Isaiah writes that God didn't make His message secret but declared "things that are right" (Isaiah 45:19). He speaks the truth.

We know where those right things are—in the Bible. When we have acknowledged God as Lord of all, and we wait patiently on Him, we can say as the psalmist did, "I will see Your face in righteousness. I shall be satisfied with Your likeness when I awake" (Psalm 17:15). God's righteousness, which at one time was threatening, becomes pleasing.

For from the creation of the world the invisible things of Him are clearly seen, have been understood by the things that are made, even His eternal power and Godhead, so that they are without excuse.

ROMANS 1:20

114. WHERE'S YOUR STRENGTH?

*But those who wait on the LORD shall renew their **strength**.*
They shall mount up with wings like eagles, they shall run
and not be weary, and they shall walk and not faint.

ISAIAH 40:31

What kind of strength do you need? Moral strength to resist sin? Strength in the midst of need? The ability to withstand deception and wicked rulers? The power to find joy in life? God can provide it all. There is no strength the Lord cannot share with us, no deception He cannot overcome, or no world leader who doesn't lie in His hands.

If temptation looms large, "Be strong in the Lord and in the power of His might. Put on the whole armor of God, that you may be able to stand against the schemes of the devil" (Ephesians 6:10–11). The Lord Jesus is your protection as you stand with Him: "In that He Himself has suffered being tempted, He is able to aid those who are tempted" (Hebrews 2:18). God never allows Satan full sway in our lives. James 4:7 promises: "Submit yourselves, therefore, to God. Resist the devil and he will flee from you."

Whether Paul was in need or had plenty, he reported, "I can do all things through Christ who strengthens me" (Philippians 4:13). Circumstances change, but God doesn't. As we call on Him for strength, He is pleased and answers that prayer.

When wicked rulers are in power, God reminds us that He can bring them down in a minute. We've seen this throughout the Old Testament and in our own day. Reading the Bible can be like reading about our own world.

Finally, Nehemiah told the Israelites, "The joy of the Lord is your strength" (Nehemiah 8:10). Where are you looking for strength in your life? You'll find it in the Lord as you wait on Him.

"Strength and wisdom are with Him. The deceived and the deceiver are His. . . . He pours contempt on princes and weakens the strength of the mighty."

Job 12:16, 21

115. UP, UP, AND AWAY

But those who wait on the LORD shall renew their strength.
*They shall mount **up** with wings like eagles, they shall run*
and not be weary, and they shall walk and not faint.

ISAIAH 40:31

Where exactly is heaven? That's hard to say, but Colossians 3:1–2 indicates it is "above" us:

> *If you then are risen with Christ, seek those things*
> *that are above, where Christ sits on the right hand of*
> *God. Set your affection on things above, not on things*
> *on the earth.*

Perhaps that's why Isaiah 40:31 depicts the healthy, joyful Christian as someone who "mounts up," who can soar like an eagle does. As we contemplate heaven, where Jesus is building us a home (John 14:1–4), where He sits at the Father's right hand, where He "always lives to make intercession" for His own (Hebrews 7:25), we rise above the dreariness of this world. We can leave all the anger and frustration and violence and insanity far below, while we ourselves live on a completely different plane.

We all prefer the mountaintop to the valley. We all want to

be "on top of things." God knows this, and He provides the way to be "up"—by waiting on Him.

If anyone ever had reason to be down, it was Jeremiah. He had warned God's people about their sin and the coming punishment, but they didn't listen. And when the Babylonians invaded Jerusalem and Judah, it was awful. His book of Lamentations drips with horror and sadness, though right in the middle he stops to say,

> *I recall this to my mind; therefore I have hope.*
> *It is because of the LORD's mercies that we are not*
> *consumed, because His compassions do not fail. They*
> *are new every morning. Your faithfulness is great.*
> *"The LORD is my portion," says my soul. "Therefore*
> *I will hope in Him." The LORD is good to those who*
> *wait for Him, to the soul who seeks Him.*
>
> LAMENTATIONS 3:21–25

If waiting on God could lift Jeremiah from his circumstances, it can certainly raise us up too.

> *For as the heaven is high above the earth,*
> *so great is His mercy toward those who fear Him.*
> PSALM 103:11

116. TEMPLE OF PRAISE

*But those who wait on the LORD shall renew their **strength**.
They shall mount up with wings like eagles, they shall run
and not be weary, and they shall walk and not faint.*

ISAIAH 40:31

Exodus 15 recounts a praise song the Hebrews sang after God rescued them from Pharaoh and destroyed the pursuing Egyptian army. God's strength had brought His people into freedom, and they praised Him for it, knowing where their salvation had come from—it would have been hard to miss the works He had done to convince Pharaoh to let them go.

They had a long walk ahead of them to the promised land, but they would not faint. God's strength was no momentary thing. The work He'd started in His nation was yet to be completed, but He would see it through.

Along the way, the Hebrews whined, complained, and failed God, but He was always faithful to His often less-than-faithful people. He understood that the way was hard and His people were frail. Though we can't use that as an excuse for failure, God is always compassionate—He wants to make His people strong, to give them joy, to help them succeed.

When has God done an amazing work in your life? How do you praise Him when He does?

Under Moses' direction, the people of Israel prepared a dwelling place for God. Of course, as Solomon said centuries later, "Behold, the heavens and heaven of heavens cannot contain You" (1 Kings 8:27). But the tabernacle was the one place on earth where God would manifest Himself to His people, and for the forty years it took them to reach Canaan, He was there. God inhabited that tent until Solomon built a permanent temple. Tabernacle or temple, it was a place to praise and honor the God who strengthens His own.

Does God have a temple of praise in your heart? Is He your strength and song?

The LORD is my strength and song, and He has become my salvation. He is my God, and I will prepare Him a dwelling, my father's God, and I will exalt Him.
EXODUS 15:2

117. ONE TESTIMONY

But those who wait on the Lord shall renew their strength.
*They shall mount up with wings like eagles, they shall **run***
and not be weary, and they shall walk and not faint.

ISAIAH 40:31

The apostle Paul needed God's strength to run his race of faith without weariness. He physically suffered for his faith (2 Corinthians 11:25; 2 Corinthians 11:24–33) and received critiques from both Gentiles and Jews (Acts 18:4–6; 2 Corinthians 10:1–2, 11:6–12). Gentile Corinthians, who made up the difficult Corinthian church, accused Paul of uncouth speech; when he was with them, they said he was too mild mannered, but when he wrote them from afar, they complained he was too bold. Nothing made the Gentile Corinthians happy, while Jews hated the fact that Paul claimed Jesus was their Messiah.

The apostle who'd had so much discouragement urged the Philippians to live in a way that showed his ministry hadn't been in vain. They did that, and Paul's ministry, which once seemed endangered, reached the world.

Faithful spiritual work can seem useless. In worldly terms, it may not appear to have done much. But the world cannot judge spiritual effectiveness. One shoe salesman, Edward Kimball, witnessed to Dwight Moody, one of his Sunday school students. Following his conversion, Moody became a very effective evangelist. Through the ministries that followed Moody's and were thus based on Kimball's testimony, other Christians brought the gospel to Billy Sunday, who also became an evangelist, and the line of ministry finally led to the conversion of Billy Graham. One moment of ministry that may have seemed a small thing brought the gospel to millions of people. Billy Graham alone preached to over 200 million people around the world.

Today you may share your faith with one person whose testimony could change many other lives. That is running your race successfully. And it begins with your waiting on the Lord.

Do all things without murmurings and arguments, that you may be blameless and harmless, the sons of God, without rebuke, in the midst of a crooked and perverse nation, among whom you shine as lights in the world, holding forth the word of life, that I may rejoice in the day of Christ that I have not run in vain, nor labored in vain.

PHILIPPIANS 2:14–16

118. FRUITFUL TREES

But those who wait on the LORD shall renew their strength.
*They shall mount up with wings **like** eagles, they shall run*
and not be weary, and they shall walk and not faint.

ISAIAH 40:31

There are lots of metaphors in scripture. The theme verse for this book uses the "with wings like eagles" metaphor. In this devotion, we'll focus on another: "He shall be like a *tree* planted by the rivers of water" (Psalm 1:3). In this case, the psalmist uses the idea of a tree to illustrate that those who soar are fruitful. That is, they produce results that build Jesus' kingdom and advance the cause and influence of it.

Similarly, in the words of Jesus, we see the metaphor of a vine that spreads branches (John 15:1–8). Jesus said He is the vine, and we are those branches. If we abide in Jesus, we will bear much fruit.

Jesus says that if His words abide in us, we will abide in Him. As we prayerfully read through His Word and then meditate on what it says (this is the idea of "waiting on the Lord"), it will take hold of our hearts and minds. It will also take deep root within our souls, blossoming into a beautiful flower that draws others to Him. If we earnestly make that our daily prayer, we will find the energy we need to soar, reflecting the sunshine of His grace on all we meet.

We will also bring forth fruit in its season. What we sow, Jesus will reap for His kingdom in His season of reaping. We sow by sharing our faith in Him with others when they ask us for a reason hope radiates from within us (1 Peter 3:15). The more we prayerfully read and meditate on His Word, the more life-giving energy He will give us to soar and sow. We will never wither on the vine.

Whatever we do to build His kingdom under His guidance and direction, it will prosper for Him. Now that is soaring!

Blessed is the man who does not walk in the counsel of the ungodly or stand in the way of sinners or sit in the seat of the scornful. But his delight is in the law of the LORD, and on His law he meditates day and night.

PSALM 1:1–2

119. WAITING IN THE SPIRIT

*But those who **wait** on the LORD shall renew their strength.*
They shall mount up with wings like eagles, they shall run
and not be weary, and they shall walk and not faint.

ISAIAH 40:31

Paul warned the Galatian church against getting caught up in the law through circumcision. Those who did that had fallen from grace, he explained, and looked to their own good works to earn them righteousness. Instead, they were to await righteousness by faith (Galatians 5:5).

How much joy would anyone get waiting for a legal righteousness? It sounds like a fairly painful way to relate to God. And Paul knew all about the law, having lived under its restrictions for most of his life. He understood that faith in Christ was far better. Old Testament Jews lived by faith and sacrifices, but the Holy Spirit did not indwell all believers as He did after Pentecost.

Now Paul hoped in the Spirit, who worked righteousness in his life and gave him the expectation of its complete fulfillment in eternity. Jesus' coming didn't abrogate the law but fulfilled it. Following His death and resurrection, the Father sent the Spirit to live within those who followed Jesus by faith.

Though the kingdom of God came through Jesus, the fulfillment of righteousness by faith still lies ahead. Between Pentecost and today, believers have waited in hope for it. But unlike most faithful Old Testament believers, we wait with the power of the Holy Spirit working in our lives.

God has given us a foretaste of righteousness in this life, but in eternity it will surround us and fill us in a way it cannot now. The wonders of that promise easily make us impatient. We long to be perfect in Christ. "Come quickly, Lord Jesus!" we may cry as our world becomes a harsher and harsher place. Be patient—He will come.

God calls us to wait until all His sheep are in the fold. Then the waiting will end, and joy will fill our hearts.

"And He shall send His angels with a great sound of a trumpet, and they shall gather together His elect from the four winds, from one end of heaven to the other."
MATTHEW 24:31

120. RUNNING IN GOD'S COMMANDMENTS

*But those who wait on the LORD shall renew their strength. They shall mount up with wings like eagles, they shall **run** and not be weary, and they shall walk and not faint.*

ISAIAH 40:31

In the classic film *Chariots of Fire*, Olympic champion Eric Liddell says, "God made me fast. And when I run, I feel His pleasure." The Lord had endowed Liddell with an extraordinary athletic ability. He used that talent to honor God and point others to Him.

Not all of us are runners. But we can all excel at the "running" God's Word describes. Running in this way means we delight in His commandments, just like the writer of Psalm 119, which includes 176 verses extolling God's Word. The Lord's instructions should be of such great value to us that we cheerfully embrace them. We should be eager to follow them and carry them out because we have come to understand their life-giving and life-enriching nature. With this kind of understanding, obedience is not a chore but a pleasure.

We realize that our heavenly Father has given us His commandments because He loves us—without limit. He knows far better than we do what is best for us. So He provides His Word for our own welfare and protection to prevent us from wandering down a road that leads away from Him. With all this in mind, we are propelled forward purposefully on the pathway that pleases Him—the pursuit He richly rewards.

I will run the way of Your commandments, when You shall enlarge my heart. Teach me, O LORD, the way of Your statutes, and I shall keep it to the end. Give me understanding, and I shall keep Your law; yes, I shall observe it with my whole heart. Make me to go in the path of Your commandments, for I delight in them.

PSALM 119:32–35

SCRIPTURE INDEX

OLD TESTAMENT

Proverbs

NEW TESTAMENT

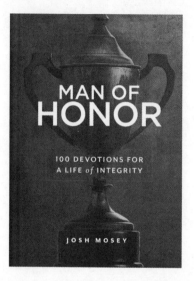